Planning and Reviewing Work Based Learning

A Practical Guide

Planning and Reviewing Work Based Learning

A Practical Guide

Karen Hardacre and Barbara Workman

LIBRI
PUBLISHING

First published in 2010 by Libri Publishing

Copyright © CEWBL

ISBN 978 1 907471 12 4

A CIP catalogue record for this book is available from The British Library

Cover design by Helen Taylor

Design by Carnegie Book Production

Printed in the UK by Ashford Colour Press

Libri Publishing
Brunel House
Volunteer Way
Faringdon
Oxfordshire
SN7 7YR

Tel: +44 (0)845 873 3837

www.libripublishing.co.uk

Contents

Foreword

Workforce development and higher level skills are critically important in the progressive rebuilding of the UK economy, in particular supporting business to meet global challenges and remain competitive.

The British further and higher education system has been highly successful in developing and delivering entry to work programmes for many years; that is, qualifying people for work at higher levels. It has not performed as well when it comes to those in work at a time when it is needed.

Nevertheless, the FE/HE sector continues to engage in giving graduates the relative chances of acquiring and maintaining different kinds of employment. However, continuous professional development, retraining, part-time provision, learning diagnostics, assessment and certification, all work based, remain marginal in university provision. Why is this the case, when the national economic and social demands are as strident as ever? Part of the story is a general lack, at a local university level, of an overall institutional work based learning strategy and as the Council for Industry and Higher Education (CIHE) says; there is a lack of relative importance attached to this type of activity, including making links with business compared with developing academic research and international standing. This could be attributed to public sector funding priorities which, until recently, have not encouraged higher education engagement in workforce development.

There is an exception to this which is Middlesex University's Institute for Work Based Learning. The Institute for Work Based Learning (IWBL) was formed in 2007 as a strategic initiative to enable the University to build upon its nationally recognised excellence in work based learning (WBL).

It was the pioneering development of work based learning at higher education level which led to the first National Centre for Work Based Learning Partnerships (NCWBLP) in 1992, now the Institute.

It is then no surprise, to find this practical book dedicated to commissioning work based learning drawing on the experience of Institute staff. This is a step-by-step guide to the commissioning, design, delivery and evaluation of work based learning, including a helpful description of work based learning characteristics and the contexts in which the learning takes place. An inclusive, collaborative and structured approach to designing work based learning programmes is encouraged. The guiding questions and activities are designed to be generic and to generate principles of engagement with learning through, at and for work.

This is a welcome contribution to the subject for all those intending to commission work based learning programmes in public or private sector, universities or further education colleges. It can also play a part in supporting workforce development at an important time by clearly explaining how to commission work based learning.

Professor Simon Roodhouse

Introduction

Origins of this book

This book has been created to act as a resource and guide for commissioners of Work Based Learning (WBL), those agencies providing it, and people learning for, through, and at work. It provides a step-by-step approach to commissioning and design, some aspects of delivery, and evaluation of WBL, offering key questions at each stage to enable organisations and individuals to scope and define robust arrangements to support successful WBL. It is likely to be of interest to those who commission Work Based Learning, work-based learners, their managers, workforce development leads, and education and training providers. The book can be read in discrete chapters, but they do cross refer and the commissioning and evaluation processes are more likely to inform the reader if these are followed through sequentially.

Some of the research on which this book is based arose from a project delivered by Karen Hardacre and Kate Schneider (2008) to determine best practice in WBL, commissioned by Skills for Health, the UK Sector Skills Council for Health. The project looked at the benefits of WBL, models in use, relevance of models to skills escalation, and any gaps in practice. The report also looked at the application of National Occupational Standards (NOS) in the context of WBL. This resulted in a literature review of WBL and its impact, a report, and the text for a web-based tool which was designed to assist in the commissioning process. The tool has formed the basis of this book, which incorporates much of the contextualising information and underpinning rationale so that it can be used as a resource for commissioners of WBL in a variety of organisations. As the information emerged initially from the Health sector, the experience is mainly from the public sector, but the principles can be transferred to any organisation that commissions WBL. Whilst this may mean that there are gaps in information for particular sectors, the book aims to be sufficiently comprehensive to enable a strategic approach to be taken to the commissioning process, so that the end result meets the organisational needs.

Much of the supporting literature from the project was developed by sectors other than health, and the messages it contains therefore have wider applicability. The resulting web-based tool looked at commissioning, design, delivery and evaluation of WBL. Clearly, most organisations interested in WBL will have an interest in these areas. All learning projects are led and managed within business, financial and management constraints and all require evaluation to determine whether the money and effort was worthwhile.

There is an emphasis on *collaboration* throughout the book. This is because we believe that effective collaboration and a positive and honest approach to partnership between employers, commissioners, providers of learning and learners themselves, delivers a better outcome for everyone. To this end, the book contains an emphasis on stakeholder approaches.

Where possible, the term 'learning' rather than 'training' has been used in the book. 'Training' as a term is widely used to indicate a short episode of teacher/trainer input, and is aimed at immediate and often practical acquisition of skills. Unless implemented immediately its value can be lost, and it is often not accompanied by the need for in-depth understanding. By contrast, learning encompasses the notion of learning as a life skill, and is aimed at embedding new skills and understanding into practice.

The contents of the chapters

Chapter One will consider WBL and how it can add value to an organisation. It will discuss a learning-cycle model of reflection that is helpful in relation to understanding WBL processes. Drawing on the research that underpins this book, eight critical success factors in WBL are described. These highlight the important components that will make WBL much more effective.

Chapter Two considers a variety of forms and resources for WBL and how these might contribute to learning at work. Some key characteristics of a learning environment at work are discussed, culminating in four approaches to WBL: skills-based learning, problem-based learning, project-based learning and social learning, all of which offer structured approaches to learning in the workplace.

Chapter Three discusses commissioning as a response to a business plan and encourages a review of the organisational outcomes required for the sector as guided and directed by local and national processes and standards. Having determined the purpose of the WBL programme, it then offers questions to help develop clarity about the purpose of the proposed programme in order to aid the commissioning process. It also gives some tips relating to costs, value for money and practicalities of setting up a WBL programme.

Chapter Four explores planning the implementation of WBL. It reflects upon those who have a contribution to make to the process and offers some key questions for different parties involved to guide the planning and scope of the WBL programmes. It discusses the value of and reasons for accreditation of a programme and how accreditation may be influenced by the assessment strategies used.

Chapter Five considers building capacity within the organisation in order that WBL can happen effectively. Roles that are required to support learning and delivery of the programme are identified and there is some further discussion about the eight critical success factors explored in the first chapter, highlighting issues that are particularly relevant for the organisation. Dissemination of learning into the organisation is also considered as a WBL learning strategy. The use of effective assessment, and how to design and deliver it, is discussed to ensure the planning process considers creating capacity in the workforce to support WBL.

The final chapter considers the evaluation of the learning programme. A stakeholder approach is advocated as this supports the main approach that this book presents, but it also briefly offers two other approaches – the 'Kirkpatrick model' (Kirkpatrick, 1994) and an 'evaluative research' approach (Robson, 2000) – that might suit particular sectors. While these are touched upon, most commissioning organisations have access to formal evaluation processes and tools, and therefore these are not explored in the same detail as the stakeholder approach.

This book offers a collaborative approach to creating, planning, implementing and evaluating a WBL programme, with the aim of providing practical guidance to assist in the process, and using a structured approach to designing the programme so that all participants are involved and included. Whilst it was generated from the public sector – in particular, the area of health – it can be adapted to suit other sectors as the guiding questions and activities are designed to be generic and to generate principles of engagement with learning through, at and for work. Our hope is that it will enable sound learning experiences at work to occur and be captured so that work and learning can become synonymous and productive in a number of ways.

References

Hardacre, K. and Schneider, K. (2008) (PSE Consulting Ltd) *Evaluating Work Based Learning report, draft tool and literature search for Skills for Health*, available from www.skillsforhealth.org.uk as at 31 March 2009

Kirkpatrick, D.L. (1994) *Evaluating Training Programmes: the four levels*, Berrett-Koehler

Robson, C. (2000) *Small Scale Evaluation*, Sage Publications Ltd

CHAPTER ONE

Why Work Based Learning?

Characteristics of Work Based Learning

WBL is increasingly used in all parts of the education sector, from supporting NVQ units, Skills for Life, apprenticeships (both Foundation and Modern Apprenticeships), and foundation and undergraduate degrees. Additionally, postgraduate programmes and credits are increasingly used within sectors or services to contribute to Master's programmes. Delivery methods vary with increasing use of e-learning packages, but many other forms of learning are included, and these are discussed in more detail in Chapter Two. WBL promotes learning that is focused on the realities of practice, service development and improving services.

Successful WBL aligns people's development with the aims and objectives of their employer, and how it is delivered, or undertaken, should be responsive and adapted to the needs and preferences of both the learner and the employer. The emphasis is on learning rather than being taught: learning is centred on the individual; it is a shared and collective activity, and as such many of us would recognise ourselves as being work-based learners.

There are many definitions of Work Based Learning (Connor, 2005). Furthermore, different parts of the education and training sector (and different employers) use the term to describe or incorporate a plethora of initiatives from higher education programmes to the delivery of apprenticeships and S/NVQs. For the purpose of this book, the key definition of WBL is *"learning that takes place for, in, and through paid and unpaid work"* (UALL, 2006). Within most sectors, WBL is interpreted as learning which focuses on the realities of practice within a theoretical and reflective framework. At university level, WBL also requires the learner to develop the skills of critical analysis, inquiry, research and development and practical application of new knowledge to work practices (www.mdx. ac.uk). Importantly WBL is not just about vocational learning, but also the development of new theoretical perspectives and critical approaches to work and practice through reflection and development of knowledge relating to the work context.

The context of learning

Most definitions of WBL these days would accept the central role of the workplace in supporting learning, with the learner as central partner. The employing organisation plays a key but flexible role, in that the focus of the learning may differ, but that varying amounts of learner input and support are negotiated between the employer and education institution. In some cases, WBL is entirely provided in-house, with little external support commissioned. Different models of WBL are explored in Chapter Two and will provide a clearer picture of which WBL approaches may be most appropriate for the type of learning required by the commissioning organisation.

Why use the Work Based Learning approach?

Employers identify a wide range of reasons for undertaking WBL, particularly around notions of flexibility. It allows for close alignment between theory and practice-based learning, in that both formal and informal learning are related to the practical work context. It can support individuals, be team-based or shared learning.

As learners, staff members are more likely to learn effectively when familiar with their surroundings, and when programmes can be tailored to meet their needs and those of the organisation rather than provided 'off the peg'. Additionally flexibility of delivery models and methods, offering a mix between classroom-based and practical learning, both on and off-site, can suit particular needs of both the organisation and the learner.

Financial benefits are often anticipated with WBL, for example, by allowing increased numbers of participants per course, and by making it easier to release staff within their own area. However, WBL is not always a cheaper option; rather, it can provide a mechanism for redirecting available funding more effectively, such as through saving on travel costs. It can allow for the elimination of unnecessary course components, such as training previously provided elsewhere or components not relevant to the work area. If well thought through, it is possible to evaluate the results of WBL in terms of future workforce performance or improvements to processes or services, as well as making best use of available organisational resources. It should be noted that WBL does not suit every type of learner. Where learning is expected to happen in the workplace, it requires a particular type of learning discipline; one that requires self-direction and individual motivation as well as the learner being inquisitive about their practice. This may not come easily to all learners, and should be taken into account when planning WBL.

Learning organisations and their contribution

Peter Senge (1990) developed the notion of the learning organisation in his book *The Fifth Discipline*. Since then, the concept of the learning organisation has gained currency, and is generally used to mean an organisation where everyone expands their capacity to learn, where learning is supported, and where results of learning are valued and acted upon. This means that by taking a proactive approach to planning and determining the type of WBL suitable for a specific organisation, and in line with its learners' needs, WBL can make a significant impact on the organisation as a whole.

WBL is ideally suited as a mechanism to support learning organisations. It allows for individual and work-centred learning, and is adaptable to provide shared learning across teams and organisations. It is capable of providing the opportunity for immediate (just-in-time) learning, and ensures that learners are central to the learning partnership, rather than subject to it. It focuses on the reality of what people do in their daily work, and encourages reflection and openness to change.

Learning cycles – taking theory to practice

A key strength of Work Based Learning is that it capitalises on experiential learning, within a structured context. The importance of experiential learning has been known for some time, and understanding of the key part played by concrete experience was developed by Kolb (1984) in his theory of experiential learning as a source of learning and development. Kolb identifies four points in the learning cycle starting with concrete experience, whereby the learner undergoes experience by 'doing' things in practice. He then reflects upon (or 'observes') that experience in terms of seeing how it is applied and what the impact of that 'doing' has been. This then leads to further thinking and the development of new ideas or concepts (abstract conceptualisation), which offers alternative solutions or strategies and which may then result in new action testing the alternatives in practice (active experimentation). According to this concept, an individual can start at any point of the learning cycle, although concrete experience is often first. This also means that much learning happens whilst 'doing' the job, but in order to capture that learning and make the most of it, the learner has to have the skills and opportunity to reflect, and also new knowledge to form ideas about alternative actions. This new knowledge may come from formal learning, such as from a classroom or learning session, from an expert in the field, or a colleague or peer who is able to inform the development of new ideas. It is not always essential for WBL to have formal taught input as there are many sources of new knowledge available to a learner–worker; and to maximise the possibilities of WBL, these other sources need to be considered. The following diagram illustrates the learning cycle concept.

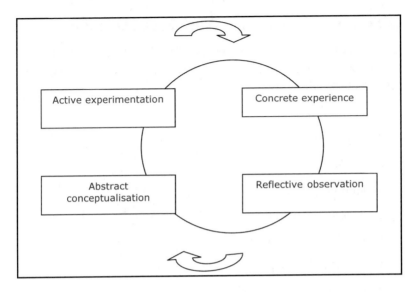

Kolb (1984) Learning Cycle

KOLB, David A.; Experiential Learning: Experience as a Source of Learning and Development; © 1984, p.42. Reprinted with the permission of Pearson Education Inc., Upper Saddle River, NJ.

For those supporting WBL, either at work or in education, facilitation of reflective activity to enable the best outcomes from the learning is a key principle. Reflection is a learnt skill which can be useful throughout an individual's working life, learning to look back over particular activities to see what influenced them, what has been learned, and how things could be done differently another time. Some people undertake regular reflection in group settings, for example in action-learning groups, in peer-review settings, or with a mentor or supervisor. Others prefer to reflect alone, perhaps using a portfolio or learning diary to support the process. Reflection is an important and powerful component of WBL, and the learning experience is richer if opportunities are taken to incorporate it.

Critical success factors in Work Based Learning

From the Skills for Health project research (PSE, 2007), eight 'critical success factors' which influence the success of Work Based Learning have been identified. These are:

1. Partnership

2. Leadership

3. Outcomes

4. Infrastructure

5. Involvement of learners

6. Facilitation and support

7. Capacity and capability

8. Evaluation.

Each of these factors is considered in further detail below.

1. Partnership

> "The relationship between the agency commissioning WBL, the agency providing work based learning (whether internal or external), and the learner is one of **partnership**, each bringing knowledge, skills, experience, capacity and resources to the table". (PSE, 2007)

Different models of WBL involve different types of partnership. Internal models, where the whole of the learning is kept in-house, will include in that partnership: managers (maybe at different levels), learning or other human resource staff, the learners themselves, and perhaps others. Where external organisations provide the learning, they are an additional partner with a stake in its success, and often different organisations pay for the learning and even have different roles simply commissioning it. Partnership working skills are therefore important with some partnerships resembling alliances, in that the partners are equal.

Identifying the right partners and keeping them involved is important, as is effective engagement and re-engagement with them. Research has demonstrated that partnerships are *built* through the seven key steps of: orientation, trust building, goal clarification, commitment, implementation, and continued high performance. These are essential to the formation and maintenance of partnerships. (http://www.edc.org/divisions/health_and_human_development_programs_hhd)

The same research shows that sustaining partnerships requires skill in persuading and negotiating, demonstrating understanding for the concerns of others, involving high levels of communication and coordination, recognising and working with the styles of others (and being able to vary one's own) and the willingness to share power when appropriate.

One of the attractions of WBL is its ability to lend itself to imaginative ways of creating and designing learning. For example, commissioning organisations themselves may be in a better position to teach about the use of the latest procedures, skills and technologies than education providers, whereas education providers may be better placed to support the learning activities and provide accreditation. The enthusiasm of employer organisations for WBL can be developed by partnerships with accrediting bodies, who will provide the currency for WBL in the form of accredited learning.

In case studies, Doncaster and Garnett (2000) identify five key criteria for successful partnerships. These are:

- Explicit learning outcomes
- Formal assessment processes
- Identification and delivery of standards
- The application of appropriate HE quality
- Enhancement processes and recognition through the award of credit or other certification.

Being explicit about the role of each partner helps to clarify expectations throughout the process of development, negotiation and implementation of a WBL programme.

2. Leadership

> "Skilled **leadership** at a senior level is required to set the direction, broker partnerships, and ensure delivery". (PSE, 2007)

The facets of effective leadership have been the subject of many debates in all sectors and it is not intended to revisit that discussion here. However, there exists a critical need for more expertise and capacity to lead and support WBL, and this includes the need for consensus about the definition and delivery of WBL. It is just beginning to be understood that specifying, supporting and evaluating WBL is a complex process, and that a range of skills and attitudes are needed to contribute to this, from contracting to relationship management to evaluation. Investment is needed in the qualities, skills, and experience required. The leadership role and responsibilities include leading colleagues and learners towards an understanding of WBL and its implications. These leadership skills are distinct from coordination skills, although they may be provided by the same person.

Project leadership and adequate administrative support are crucial to assist introduction, delivery, monitoring and successful implementation of the programme. Organisations without the capacity to employ these skills in a dedicated role need to look at different ways of providing them consistent with the needs and scale of the learning activity. Occasionally steering committees can perform this function, or education development departments, but the key ingredient is to provide oversight and support to the project leader. However, administrative support cannot be underestimated, particularly in terms of a fixed contact point for learners' and managers' enquiries and external stakeholders.

3. Outcomes

> "Learning **outcomes** need to be predicated on the learning needs of the individual and the organisation; learning must be relevant, and it must have the opportunity for immediate application". (PSE, 2007)

Outcomes should be based on what learners are required to do and to know at the end of the programme. They must make clear what changes of behaviour are expected at the end of the learning.

Ensuring that WBL is relevant can be aided through the use of competences or standards to map needs against demand, and by learning providers matching their ability to support delivery of the competences required. The greater the clarity about what is required, the easier it is to ensure its relevance. For example, what support or elements of the learning can be provided in-house and, ideally, how soon are they needed and at what level?

WBL needs to be timely. Delivering a two-year learning programme may suit the longer-term skill needs of an individual, but is unlikely to be sufficiently useful to solve more pressing needs in the organisation. Thought should be given to the order of the learning and whether it can be designed incrementally to deliver urgent needs immediately and longer-term goals over a specific period of time. Different providers of learning can offer higher or lower level (academic or vocational) solutions, and may offer longer or shorter versions. Meeting professional body or government directions may direct the timetable but should not override the quality of the outcomes.

Doncaster (2000), Garnett (2000) and West (2000) all argue that the quality of the learning is not dependent on the quality of the learning experience, but on the quality of the process of reflection in relation to the agreed learning outcomes – i.e. that the most effective learning results from reflective practice about what has been learned. They suggest that employers must have a more central and continuing role in ongoing monitoring and evaluation of learning outcomes. This indicates that the commissioner must be fully aware of what is required at the outset to ensure that organisational needs are not subsumed. Additionally, a record of employee development should be maintained to ensure that their performance reflects the learning and development that they have undertaken. This will also demonstrate the extent to which WBL has been effective in meeting required outcomes (King, 2007). The chapter on commissioning explores in detail how to arrive at effective outcomes for WBL.

4. Infrastructure

> "The learner needs to be supported by an **infrastructure** which offers clarity, support, protected time, supervision, funding, assessment, and recognition". (PSE, 2007)

Ensuring the quality of the learning experience involves a complex infrastructure to support the learning and this complexity may not be initially apparent. Contrary to received wisdom, WBL is not an easy option and may require more proactive support and intervention from the organisation than standard education or learning. Work-based learners benefit greatly from staying in their jobs, as they have the opportunity to ground and contextualise their learning in practice. But this is not the same as learning whilst working full time, juggling competing demands of earning and learning. WBL can easily fail if effective learner support is not available. Learners need time to reflect on their learning, to engage in relevant activities, and will benefit from appropriate facilitation and supervision provided from the workplace. They may need placements or shadowing opportunities, job swaps, and tuition time away from work. WBL project managers will need to consider carefully the infrastructure requirements of each WBL programme, review them as necessary, and possibly even formalise mentoring or supervisory processes, or the procedures for back-filling time release for learners.

Additionally, funding mechanisms need to be clarified so that there is equity across organisations or departments supporting learners and agreeing payment for courses, or time out to attend study.

5. Involvement of learners

> "Successful work based learning projects make learners a full partner in the learning". (PSE, 2007)

Adult learners are known to undertake learning in a different way to children and their experience plays a key part in the learning activity. It helps to motivate the learner if the new learning is relevant to their need to know about something (Knowles et al., 2005). Involving them in their own learning and getting them to participate in the planning and delivery of it can help the worker–learner to participate and engage more effectively.

Undertaking a project at work can be a very successful approach to WBL. It does not need to involve an external provider, but does need to be facilitated in order that the learning is effective and transferable. Many WBL programmes will feature an opportunity to undertake a WBL project and workers may already be undertaking work projects which can then be put into an educational framework. This will maximise the learning from them, both in terms of providing external recognition through accreditation, and also by developing additional academic skills in executing the project. Undertaking learning that is directly related to work provides motivation and relevance for the worker–learner and therefore stimulates them to be fully engaged in the learning process (Knowles et al., 2005).

WBL projects enable:

- Learners' goals to be aligned so that there is a synergy between personal goals and organisational goals

- Engagement in constant real-time activity and critical review and feedback

- Others to grow with and through the project process.

Waddington and Marsh (1998) and Bond and Wilson (2000) offer some useful ideas in exploring further the notions of shared responsibility for planning and enabling the learning process as key features in making

WBL work. Crucially, organisations need to plan what they will do with staff who may be unsuccessful in their learning, as it may result in them requiring remedial help at work or transfer to new positions for which their skills are more suited.

6. Facilitation and support

> "WBL needs to be **facilitated and supported**: line managers, clinical tutors, coaches, practice facilitators, assessors play an essential role in work based learning". (PSE, 2007)

Facilitating WBL is an ongoing process. Time needs to be dedicated to supporting learners once they are in place. Decisions will be required about who is going to provide the kind of support required; usually it is a combination of both the commissioner and the provider of the learning, and may involve managers, or a human resources department, and possibly the unions. Organisations that are offering the work-based-practice element of the learning are often best placed to contribute most of these roles. The provider of learning may also need to provide learning for these support roles, particularly if work-based assessment is required.

The motivation of learners to learn can be supported by an effective facilitation style. Sandars (2006) argues that the 'net generation' presents a challenge to WBL, citing the interactive and immediate features through which the internet generation learns, in environments that are rich in image and sound, and which are often preferred to those predominantly composed of text. This group may prefer to be actively engaged in tasks rather than reading or writing about events and the motivation to learn comes from being actively involved and by attempts to answer questions that arise during a task. This clearly implies a lot about the style of facilitation required.

WBL promotes the idea of the active learner, synthesising an array of information from widely dispersed resources, with the educator's role changing from that of a provider of information to that of a facilitator, providing guidance, steering the learning activity, and supplementing the worker–learner's knowledge base with additional learning activities. At university level this develops other skills of critical inquiry, analysis and evaluation. Additionally, it should be recognised that there are a number of different learning styles (e.g. Kolb, 1984) which need to be accommodated in the variety of learning activities so that all learners have an opportunity to learn in a way that suits their individual style. Hence the role of facilitator is best allocated to someone with appropriate training, experience and inclination for the role.

Tennant (2005) offers some useful direction on the role of modern workplace facilitators as arbiters, guides, and assessors of performance. They should be equipped to support learners to:

- Analyse the workplace experience

- Learn from others

- Act without all the facts available

- Choose from multiple courses of action

- Learn about organisational culture

- Use a wide range of resources and activities as learning opportunities

- Understand competing and varied interests in shaping of work and professional identity

- Be active in seeking learning opportunities.

Facilitators should also be able to supplement the learner's knowledge with new knowledge or resources and understand the context of the workplace with its potential learning opportunities.

7. Capacity and capability

"Organisations need the **capacity and capability** to harness the opportunities that work based learning brings; it is a process that must be supported, sponsored and led in the workplace by people who have both the time and the competence to do so". (PSE, 2007)

The capacity of the organisation to provide learning in-house and the capability of its staff to support it are critical to success. Most learning is an expensive investment and therefore requires sound project management. Organisations need not only to lead and support, but also to link learning to career development and organisational growth. Staff may be developed beyond their roles and their new skills may be useful elsewhere within the company sharing them more widely within the organisational context.

Some organisations 'contract' their learners to do this, and regularly involve them in sharing their learning with appropriate colleagues. Others keep updated skills banks for all staff, and use the information these generate. This is a cost-effective way of recognising expertise available to other staff, but also for developing in-house learning opportunities, rather than duplicating expensive learning programmes.

Capacity is not just about the time to plan, organise and manage WBL. It can also be about having the time, staff and systems in place to make the best out of the investment in the long term. Continuous Professional Development (CPD), for example, can be very effective through WBL as it can be thought of in terms of outcomes, rather than inputs. Recognition that the workplace offers learning opportunities at all levels provides a vehicle for developing and accrediting knowledge that is already available to the workforce (Shaw and Green, 1999). Therefore involving experienced staff to develop others through work can be a cost-effective way of providing CPD through WBL and developing staff capacity.

8. Evaluation

> "Realistic, meaningful and achievable methods for **evaluating** learning and service outcomes need to be developed and implemented in practice, in order fully to realise the potential of WBL". (PSE, 2007)

PSE's (2007) research demonstrated that much evaluation of WBL still tends to be conducted at a basic level, focusing on the 'how was it for you' factor or the number of learner completions. Learning interventions of any sort should be considered in relation to the original aims of the learning, and outcomes should be evaluated in relation to the original aims.

Evaluation is an underdeveloped area in all learning and development, and the evaluation of WBL is no exception. Surprisingly, most organisations do not routinely collect data to ascertain whether their investment was effective and whether they could learn from the process for future. Like all management activities, evaluation must be fit for purpose. This means matching the complexity and level of the evaluation to the size, scale and importance of the learning originally commissioned. It is not a good use of resources to undertake large-scale, multi-layered evaluation of WBL programmes, unless the original learning was of critical importance to business outcomes. Equally, it is not difficult or especially time consuming to find out valuable information about the success of the learning by thinking in advance of what information might be needed and who might know it. The key here is to consider evaluation practicalities before starting the learning, and ideally when planning to commission WBL. The complexity of the evaluation process is addressed in more detail in Chapter Six.

This chapter has summarised some of the crucial elements to be considered when planning WBL for successful learning in the workplace. These are elaborated upon more fully in the rest of the chapters.

References

Armsby, P. and Costley, C. (2000) 'Research Driven Projects', in Portwood, D. and Costley, C. (2000) *Work based Learning and the University: New Perspectives and Practices*, SEDA paper 109, Birmingham

Bond, C. and Wilson, V. (2000) 'Bridging the Academic and Vocational Divide – a Case Study on Work Based Learning in the UK NHS', published in *Innovations in Education & Training International*

Connor, H. (2005) *Workforce Development and Higher Education*, London: Council for Industry and Higher Education

Doncaster, K. (2000) 'Recognising and Accrediting Learning and the development of Reflective Thinking', in Portwood, D. and Costley, C. (2000) *Work based Learning and the University: New Perspectives and Practices*, SEDA paper 109, Birmingham

Doncaster, D. and Garnett, J. (2000) 'Effective Work Based Learning Partnerships: two case studies from Middlesex University', *Education through Partnership*, 4 (1): 18–24, Anglia Polytechnic University

Education Development Centre, inc., USA, www.edc.org, accessed February 2007

Garnett, J. (2000) 'Organisational Culture and the Role of Learning Agreements', in Portwood, D. and Costley, C. (2000) *Work based Learning and the University: New Perspectives and Practices*, SEDA paper 109, Birmingham

Hardacre, K. and Schneider, K. (2008) (PSE Consulting Ltd) *Evaluating work based learning report, draft tool and literature search for Skills for Health*, available from www.skillsforhealth.org.uk as at 31 March 2009

King, M. (2007) *Workforce development: how much engagement do employers have with higher education? A review of the evidence on employer demand*, Council for Industry and Higher Education, http://www.cihe-uk.com/publications.php

Kirkpatrick, D.L. (1994) *Evaluating Training Programmes: the four levels*, Berrett-Koehler

Knowles, M.S., Holton, E.F. and Swanson, R. (2005) *The Adult Learner*, 6th edition, Butterworth Heinemann, London

Kolb, D.A. (1984) *Experiential Learning: Experience as a Source of Learning and Development*, Financial Times/Prentice Hall (1 January 1984)

PSE (2007) *A Review of Work Based Learning in the UK Health Sector*, produced by PSE Consulting Ltd for Skills for Health, October 2007

Robson, C. (1999) *Small Scale Evaluation,* Sage Publications Ltd

Sandars, J. (2006) 'Work based learning: a social network perspective', *Work Based Learning in Primary Care*, 3, 4–12

Senge, P.M. (1990) *The Fifth Discipline – the Art and Practice of the Learning Organisation*, Broadway Business

Shaw, M. and Green, H. (1999) 'Continuing Professional Development: emerging trends in the UK', *Quality Assurance in Education*, 7 (3), 169–76

Tennant, M. (2005) *Psychology and adult learning* (3rd edition), London: Routledge

UALL (2006) *Learning for Health Improvement – A practical Guide for the workplace*, the UK Universities Association for Lifelong Learning

Waddington, K. and Marsh, L. (1998) 'Work based learning in a multigrade, multiskilled group: an action research perspective', *Managing Clinical Nursing*, 2, 101–4

West, J. (2000) 'Higher Education and employment: opportunities and limitations in the formation of skills in a mass higher education system', *Journal of Vocational Education and Training*, Vol. 52, No. 4, December, pp. 573–88 (16)

Websites

http://www.edc.org/divisions/health_and_human_development_programs_hhd, 'Developing Alliances to Improve Health and Education: Reflections of Leaders from EDC's Health and Human Development Programs', Education Development Centre, Massachusetts, website

www.mdx.ac.uk, Middlesex University IWBL website

CHAPTER TWO

What is Work Based Learning?

This chapter will provide an overview of the commonest forms of WBL and consider how they each impact on workplace, learners and organisation in relation to the support required and the facilitation of learning. Different learning activities that help learning to happen at work will be considered, particularly in relation to developing staff outside formal learning or education programmes. Four particular learning approaches in the workplace are discussed in some detail: project-based learning, problem-based learning, practical skills training and social learning.

Nine types of WBL as used in Further Education (FE) and Higher Education (HE) are summarised below from key literature (Brennan and Little, 1996; 2006; Nixon et al., 2006) and most WBL activities can be attributed to at least one of these, although not all fulfil the definition of WBL in HE as outlined in Chapter One.

1. **In-house training** – this includes apprenticeships, NVQ awards and local training provision, such as IT skills, which contribute to the job role. These are usually commissioned by the employer and types of WBL that may arise from these courses are considered in more detail below.

2. **Sandwich year** – involves full-time work for a year as part of a degree programme. This is unlikely to be commissioned from an employer and is therefore not fully explored in this chapter. However, the learning opportunities that arise in the workplace are relevant to those on sandwich placements.

3. **Vocational placements** – these enable learning on aspects of professional work, and may include long or short placements specifically linked to vocations or professions, such as performing arts, journalism and psychology courses where specific vocational skills are learnt and practised. Learners may have specific objectives to achieve, or projects to conduct whilst on placement so the suggestions relating to project-based learning may be applicable.

4. **Vocational courses** – these are usually part of professional programmes, with the outcomes determined by professional bodies rather than an employer, so are not further explored in this chapter, although general guidance regarding learning from work will be relevant. Such courses include, for example, medicine, nursing and teacher education.

5. **General work experience** – may be within a programme of study and involve short-term placements to get a flavour of the work with specific outcomes to be achieved. It may arise as part of a formal education programme, and can involve learners at any level from school or FE college through to HE awards. The opportunities to learn will come under the general guidance to learning in the workplace and so this will not be explored more fully in the chapter.

6. **Learning from part-time work** – this offers the opportunity to learn employability skills and to support or complement full-time study. There may be some relevance or applicability to current studies. Again, this may be relevant to workers from school age upwards, but is not a formal way of working and learning although the discussion related to social learning is relevant.

Any or all of these six approaches may not carry accreditation or recognition outside the workplace. Recent studies by the CBI (2008; 2009) recognise that learning on the job can be very effective, but also that a large proportion of employees do not have formal academic qualifications that are transferable to other organisations. Learning to acquire work related skills may be included in all approaches, but not all will include recognition of critical and analytical thinking skills as expected or assessed in HE. However, the following approaches do consider these academic developments.

7. **Part-time study, provider (HE/FE) specifies content** – usually the learner is a full-time worker and the part-time study course is based on the current work role, such as an MBA or BTEC award. In order to maximise learning from the programme it will be closely related to a subject discipline such as hospitality, tourism or management. The course may be framed by professional-body accreditation, which focuses the subject matter. Work will provide the context and focus for learning, but the links between the course and the work activities may not be made explicit by the educator. Assessment strategies such as a work-focused project will aim to draw the work and academic learning together.

8. **Part-time study, employer contributes to content** – the learner is a full-time worker, and the course is designed in conjunction with their employer, with the employer possibly delivering some or all of the programme. Foundation degrees are a current example of this approach. The employer may contribute to the assessment activities or specific skills such as laboratory work, practice experience or structured rotational placements through departments. Learning will be specific to the work role and will underpin work activities, and is a mix of theory and practical approaches. This approach is likely to draw on a number of WBL methods discussed in this chapter.

9. **Part-time study, content negotiated by the learner** – the learner undertakes a study programme that is individually negotiated to meet their WBL needs in the workplace, and the focus of their study is their own work activities. It may involve some joint assessment between work and university, or recognition and accreditation of prior experiential learning. It may include informal learning, such as solving work problems or undertaking work projects or attendance at conferences, or formal training. The learner will need to make the connections between these informal and formal learning events, possibly with assistance by their facilitator, mentor or tutor.

These three types of WBL are likely to have academic accreditation in some form or other.

Numbers 1, 6, 7 and 8 of these programme types have different approaches to learning which are worth considering in more detail as these will inform the choice of approach to a commissioned WBL programme. These WBL approaches can be viewed as a 'work-based continuum' (Workman, 2003; Costley and Armsby, 2006), offering a spectrum of flexible WBL approaches. Each approach meets the needs of the individual learner and the employer differently and involves different sorts of support and learning activities at various junctures. Table 2.1 summarises this. (See the end of this chapter.)

In-house training courses

These tend to be employer-driven learning as the skills learnt will reflect the organisation's needs and requirements, for example skills in certain areas such as IT, recruitment or management. Apprenticeships and NVQ awards will require specific learning for the role that workers are doing, and may involve competence assessment to determine fitness for practice; consequently they form the basis for in-house training. Other in-house learning may not include assessment and therefore may not have implications of success or failure for the worker's job. To ensure that new learning has been incorporated into practice, some in-house courses may require demonstration of outcomes with confirmation of achievement, so requiring supervision and mentoring on return to work. Consequently supervisors and mentors need to be trained to provide support and assessment. Additionally, specific competences and criteria against which to assess competency may need to be developed, which is a considerable investment of organisational time and expertise. These competences may be developed in-house, or may be based on National Occupational Standards (NOS) or professional-body requirements.

In–house training can be accredited by education providers to offer a progression route to other learning. For example, accreditation of an apprenticeship training programme may lead to an arrangement with a local FE college for progression onto a foundation degree, and include a time reduction for successful achievement of the in-house programme. This is both attractive to the learner and the organisation as it offers a route to further qualifications whilst at work without having to take personal time out to study. This can be a great motivator as it provides opportunities for those staff who would normally discount themselves from further education due to family or other commitments. In-house training is the responsibility and the property of the organisation rather than the education provider, but can work well as a joint venture, particularly if accredited.

In–house training can be shaped by several factors. The sector sets the context and the learning agenda, for example, as in engineering or hospitality. It may be guided by professional-body requirements and offer flexible delivery in terms of time and location. The assessment may focus on skills, including soft skills such as communications or attitudes as well as practical skills that are specific to the work context. The employer must identify the learning requirements for the job and provide learning support, focusing on enabling the learner to succeed and progress. Knowledge is transferred from those with the experience to those who lack it and is directed by a teacher. The learning is likely to be vocationally orientated and may adopt a training style, rather than an educative approach.

Part-time study, provider (HE/FE) specifies content

Usually the learner is a full-time worker and the part-time study course is based on the current work role, such as an MBA, BTEC or professional-body award, which is aligned to the work role. The learner is likely to be studying in order to develop their subject knowledge of the practice area, so the programme is specific to their work discipline. The emphasis is on meeting the educational provider's requirements with the learner expected to make links between theory and work applications with some educational direction and support. The learning will be discipline based and delivered by subject specialists in order to meet the knowledge expectations in the subject. Time out of the workplace for formal and informal study may be required.

Some of the learning may emphasise the development of professional and problem-solving skills through becoming a reflective practitioner, with the acquisition of reflective skills on and in practice, together with developing academic skills of critical analysis, investigation, synthesis and evaluation.

As the learner becomes more experienced they will be expected to develop increasing autonomy and self-direction in their learning. The focus will be on gaining new knowledge for practice, targeting the workplace in general rather than a given organisation, so the learner's level of achievement will be shaped by their own sphere of practice and academic capabilities. The learner should be learning 'how to learn' so that learning can continue beyond the formal taught activities, using the skills of inquiry and critique in their daily work practice.

Part-time study, employer contributes to content

The learner is a full-time worker with the course designed in conjunction with their employer, who may even deliver some or all of the programme, for example by joint assessment or through work-rotation experiences. The learning is likely to be directed by work and/or professional-body requirements and the support that the learner receives will be focused on the learning that must be acquired for the organisational sector. The assessment will focus on both the knowledge and skills that the employer wants the worker–learner to achieve, and may include 'sitting by Nellie', where skills are demonstrated and learnt through mentoring and supervised practice.

The delivery of the learning may be partially in the workplace, and partially through formal teaching, either on or off the work location, and involving an education or learning provider. For example, new skills may be learned through simulated activities or formal taught classes. The worker–learner will need a supervisor–assessor and mentor in order to gain confidence and expertise with learning support focusing on the learner's need to apply it in practice. The teacher will need to be familiar with the sector's requirements in terms of what knowledge is appropriate and the best delivery methods. The learner will need to become self-directed in seeking out learning opportunities and practise to consolidate new skills; but much of the learning process will be directed by others, usually experts in the workplace. This learning is closely associated with the context to which it relates and may include some in-house training, but it could be accredited and recognised externally to ensure transferability within the organisational sector.

Planning time out for learning, supervision and assessment in practice and preparing supervisors and assessors will require additional planning for this WBL approach. Such activities may be absorbed into an individual's workload, or distinct support roles in the workplace may need to be created to provide learning support at crucial moments in the programme.

Part-time study, content negotiated by the learner

This is where the learner, who is also a full-time worker, undertakes a study programme that is individually created to meet their WBL needs in the workplace, with the focus of their study being their work. Usually this includes a learning audit at the outset which identifies the individual's personal learning and development needs in line with their professional or organisational requirements. The knowledge required is specific to them as an individual and may not be appropriate for another colleague, as it centres on work activities such as a specific project, problem or role.

The employer may be involved, with some direct input in relation to the learning required, or in agreeing the focus of the study. This will be in relation to the employer's agenda for the individual as required by the organisation. New knowledge will be gained by the learner as they focus on what they as individuals need to know. The learner may also uncover new knowledge created in practice by others, particularly if they are undertaking a project or involved in a corporate work matter. The learning focus is negotiated and is often across disciplines, generating personal skill and knowledge development. It may include new contextual learning, such as who to seek out in order to solve a work problem, or where specific information is held and how to manage it. Delivery is flexible and may not be formal, involving self-directed investigation in order to seek out information.

Academic skills such as critical analysis of practice will be developed, with the learner challenging some received wisdom or beliefs that are taken for granted within the organisation. A university is usually involved in acting as a catalyst to help capture and create new knowledge by recognising and accrediting it, possibly through Accreditation of Prior Experiential Learning (APEL), Recognition of Prior Learning (RPL) or work projects.

These are learning processes that are incorporated into an HE programme of study, and the learner brings his/her personal learning to the academic programme to be recognised and accredited, and supplemented by new knowledge from the programme of study. The academic role will be to facilitate learning rather than delivering knowledge content, due to its individualisation.

Reflection-on-action and reflection-in-action (Schön, 1987) will be integrated into the learning process to consolidate the transformation of the learning experience into personal and professional learning. On completion, 'learning to learn' skills will be gained which remain through the rest of the learner's career to inform his/her future personal development. The learner may not need a mentor or supervisor in the workplace, but may benefit from someone at work or in their practice community offering support and discussion opportunities. If learners are self-employed they may look to other professionals in the same or similar field to aid in their reflection and learning, potentially impacting a wider sphere of practice.

Tailoring an individual's learning to their personal and organisational need is a distinct advantage of negotiated learning. By focusing on the workplace and work activities it requires less time out for formal learning input. However, it also requires study time for thinking, reflection and personal self-directed study. It can be combined with formal taught sessions that do require study leave, but other professional activities such as conference attendance, leadership activity or staff development days can contribute to the overarching learning experience, facilitated by critical reflection to capture personal learning.

Learning resources

Where learning is designed to occur within a workplace, learning resources need to be available. These can include access to:

- IT and the internet
- Professional literature and journals
- Organisational policy and procedure documents or intranet sources

- E-learning activities
- Open or distance learning activities and resources
- Library facilities
- Skills labs, practical suites, simulation areas
- Quiet study areas or discussion areas where groups can be facilitated in seminars, workshops or action learning sets
- Experts and colleagues.

These may require some significant investment by the organisation in order to provide appropriate and adequate resources. A partnership with educational providers is often preferred as that will include access to some of these resources. However, some of these facilities are appropriate whatever form of learning and development is preferred, in order that workers can access further educational development informally and routinely. Some organisations may wish to develop their own online learning programmes for staff development, particularly where the learning programmes need to be accessible irregularly in quiet moments or lunch breaks and when a cohort may not be viable for regular delivery. It is worth noting that some education providers will have suitable learning online which cannot be accessed by workers through the organisational IT systems due to firewall protection. This may need to be considered when commissioning programmes, together with compatibility and virtual storage space within IT systems.

Ways to learn at and through work

Learning can happen if there is a suitable learning environment at work. However, not all learning experiences at work are positive. Individuals are more likely to say that they have learnt from a negative experience than a positive one, which can overshadow the benefits of learning at work. A good learning environment at work can be created by the leadership in the department or organisation, especially if they consider learning as important and have themselves experienced higher-level learning outside the organisation.

Previous research in the nursing profession in the 1980s identified key leadership styles and characteristics that make a good learning environment at work. These include:

- *A positive approach to learners*: interest in the learner, being approachable, helpful and kind, with awareness of essential learning and support needs.

- *Team working*: inclusion in a team and support from other members fosters learning. Individuals feel able to ask questions and seek guidance from others. Managing team relations and aiming for a positive and appreciative work environment, valuing everyone's contribution.

- *Management style*: effective, flexible and responsive management where all staff are expected to learn from work and where learners are given additional responsibility in order to stretch and develop them. However, giving responsibility should be managed consistently as retrieving delegated work, changing a decision without discussion or following inadequate support, can cause a fall in self-confidence, negatively impacting work performance.

- *Provision of support for learning*: mentors and supervisors are trained and in place. Learning opportunities are identified, made accessible and promoted, including planned learning time. Questioning and discussion is welcomed and accommodated, and ideas integrated into practice.

- *Management of stress in the workplace*: high levels of stress reduce the ability of the learner to learn or function properly. It can affect work performance and may affect health. Support, consistent leadership and effective management provide a stable environment which can be effective in facilitating learning at work.

- *Communication networks*: effective communications within a department or organisation can clarify expectations and communicate forthcoming events that might enhance learning. However, lack of communication can disempower individuals. Miscommunication and assumptions about others' expectations are often at the root of difficulties in the work environment, and both work and learning can be adversely affected if mismanaged.

There are a number of ways learning can occur at work, but there are four key modes that may be useful to consider when commissioning WBL programmes. Each one of these involves a range of learning activities which will be elaborated upon further below. These are:

1. Skills-based learning

2. Problem-based learning

3. Project-based learning

4. Social learning.

1. Skills-based learning

A wide range of skills are learnt though work and include practical skills such as manipulating equipment, soft skills such as communication or negotiation, or performative skills such as recruiting and interviewing staff or managing meetings. Most skills will need some explanation of their purpose and underpinning rationale. This may need to be delivered outside the work environment to enable acquisition of baseline knowledge in an area where discussion can be held out of earshot of clients or other colleagues. Practical skills will need demonstration and practise in a safe or simulated environment so that the learner has opportunities to become dextrous and skilled before being exposed in the workplace. Learning practical skills needs a teacher who can demonstrate the whole skill, break it down into manageable chunks, and provide positive reinforcement as the learner gains confidence and dexterity through practise. The opportunity to practise regularly and use the skill immediately will also reinforce the learning.

Performative skills – such as managing meetings – need training initially outside the workplace, followed by practise through observing or shadowing others, and using best-practice guidance and local policies to support and direct procedures. Feedback during the process from skilled practitioners is extremely useful, so linking up with senior colleagues or mentors is valuable, particularly in a shadowing capacity. A typical model might be in-house training and simulation with theoretical input and discussion, followed by shadowing a real event with a skilled practitioner taking the lead. This can be reversed so that the learner takes the lead with the expert providing support. When the learner is confident s/he can then go solo, but with access to a mentor or supervisor to check issues or be affirmed in practice during a learning period. Similarly, learning soft skills such as communication or negotiation may start in a learning environment, but be honed through actual use. There may be opportunities for simulated practise, but also role modelling (see 4 below) can be used through observing skilled practitioners.

To summarise, skills-based learning requires:

- A safe place to learn

- Supervision in practice

- Opportunities to get things wrong and to perfect performance through practise

- Feedback and reinforcement of good practice

- Elimination of poor performance or bad practice. This can be difficult to achieve as slipping back into old ways has to be averted.

Regular positive feedback and affirmation followed by reinforcement of good practice, initially frequently, but as time goes on less frequently, will maintain new learning. Skills-based learning is often associated with vocational learning but is also relevant for specific professional qualifications such as medicine, dentistry, and management which also require HE-level academic skills and knowledge.

2. Problem-based learning

Much informal and experiential learning happens through solving problems at work. This process can be formalised by the use of critical incident analysis, or review of a work activity, as in some organisations which routinely debrief after an event to capture the learning from it. This is facilitated by a few choice questions to analyse the situation, such as: what worked and why? What was not effective and why? Capturing the learning from critical incident analysis can lead to action-based learning, which can address practice issues.

Another method of learning from a problem is for an individual to be involved in a task group devised to deal with a problem that needs to be addressed, or in reviewing a work process. The depth and extent of the learning depends on the individual's personal capabilities and organisational role, but it can be a very powerful method. It tends to involve a number of colleagues and possibly other departments, thus extending the learner's knowledge of the organisation and other colleagues across disciplines which can be useful in raising awareness of internal politics.

Sometimes an external or internal consultant may be brought in to deal with the problem, and working alongside them can provide useful learning for a worker–learner. Using this experience, they can then problem solve something similar another time, with consequent reduction in costs to the organisation or department. This is a factor that is worth considering when recruiting consultants to advise in the workplace and it is worth finding an internal person to work alongside the consultant to learn for the future. It will extend the worker's capabilities and provide a new resource for the department.

An example of using a problem-solving approach that had far-reaching effects beyond the original problem was one where recruitment and retention of junior nurses in a mental health trust was a problem for the hospital. To deal with a high vacancy rate, the nursing director commissioned a learning programme for newly qualified staff. This included rotation experience in three different sorts of mental health facilities and the upgrading of their education award to a Bachelor's degree at the end of the two-year experience, by providing specifically designed and accredited components from an education provider. This worked well and recruitment and retention improved. However, the knock-on effect was that the managers from the rotation areas began to feel unappreciated, as they were not as well-qualified as the junior staff, although they had years of experience in dealing with challenging issues at work and had undertaken significant changes and projects as part of their work roles for the organisation. In response, a further course was provided for them to enable recognition of the experience they had gained, using the WBL negotiated study approach, and slowly they began to gain qualifications and confidence in their abilities, achieving academic qualifications that reflected their capabilities. Further details and an account of the full impact upon the trust can be found at http://www.nurserotation.com/.

This demonstrates that two different approaches to WBL can be used to meet organisational needs. The newly qualified staff had their learning needs prescribed and directed by their employer to meet the organisational agenda. The experienced managers identified their own learning needs through personal learning audits and individually designed learning pathways. The organisation learnt a lot about valuing staff and providing appropriate professional development.

3. Project-based learning

Project-based learning is quite a common approach to WBL. Many workers are already involved in projects at work that are prescribed for them, and the opportunity to have recognition and support by HE or FE through learning new thinking and analytical skills gives them additional tools for the future. Projects are also relevant to employers who may have external commissions to fulfil, or need to plan work in project cycles.

A summary of the characteristics of WBL projects drawn from the literature (Armsby and Costley, 2000; Garnett, 2005) suggests that these can:

- Be real-work-based projects that are already being undertaken in the workplace

- Be real-time, real-work projects, and therefore fit for purpose

- Be triggered by the need to solve a work-based problem, or review or evaluate an aspect of work practice, or introduce a new procedure

- Develop critical awareness of research and inquiry issues

- Involve learning practical project-management skills

- Develop new knowledge as intellectual capital for the organisation

- Reflect the organisational context and culture

- Be organisational research, structured by an academic approach

- Result in a product of value to the organisation.

Not all projects are research orientated, but the learning comes from defining the project, planning, implementing and managing the process and evaluating the experience. Those projects with a research element may find that there are ethical issues that arise from conducting research at work which can raise particular dilemmas for the worker–researcher. The ethical issues reflect the human dimensions of the organisation, professional-body considerations and, most importantly, organisational issues such as the nature of the business, the intellectual property of the organisation and the role of the worker–learner as an insider and as a researcher. WBL projects can be undertaken individually or collaboratively as in the workplace. They may produce a product such as policy development, new resources for practice or protocols, etc. These are generated from the organisation's own practitioners and consequently reflect its human and intellectual capital. Among the greatest assets of an organisation are the knowledge and skills of its workers, clients and structures in the form of human, intellectual and structural capital (Garnett, 2007). A WBL project can collate a significant amount of collaborative knowledge, which is then available to share with others.

4. Social learning

This approach also involves role modelling and learning through observing how others act and behave. It is very powerful but can result in poor learning as well as effective learning. Bandura (1977; 1986) was a proponent of social learning theory and explains it in terms of how individuals interact with their environment. Learning in this way can be as effective as through trial and error. By watching the behaviour of experts and the result of that behaviour in a given situation, learners are able to adopt appropriate behaviours at work which reflect work cultures and professional norms. Social learning is powerful when learning skills such as customer care, professional attributes and management skills. It also helps workers adapt to a new work environment by finding out what sort of behaviour gets a positive response from colleagues, and how to adjust their actions in the light of verbal or body-language responses.

Social learning is also a powerful teacher when individuals go to a new workplace or are on work experience. Individuals automatically adapt their behaviour according to the responses their behaviour evokes from the group they are in. So, those who supervise individuals on work experience will be conscious of encouraging appropriate associated work behaviour such as time keeping, use of language and appropriate work attitudes. Encouraging professional norms at work is a way of social learning.

The influence of social learning cannot be underestimated, but nor can it be expected to happen automatically as exposure to good practice does not guarantee that positive attributes will be absorbed and adopted. Mentors and supervisors at work can model appropriate behaviour and good practice, but may need to direct the learner to observe it and then reinforce good practice. For example, when dealing with a customer, the mentor may suggest that the learner watches how the mentor handles the situation and then discuss with them afterwards what approaches and responses worked and why. Secondments to different departments may facilitate social learning but will be more effective if the secondee has been alerted to look out for particular attributes, knowledge and skills to acquire.

Learning through work activities

Learning through work activities can include a very wide range of activity as outlined here. Effective learning needs to have some planning and structure so that what is intended to be learnt actually is learnt, otherwise it can be a random, incomplete and incomprehensible experience. These approaches will contribute to a good learning experience, together with making expectations and standards explicit. Consequently, when planning WBL, the best approach to the learning for the outcome capabilities must be considered at the outset.

Recognition of what has been learnt through assessment is also important to maintain standards. E-learning may be part of the WBL approach but it is essential to identify what appropriate methods of learning are available to achieve the required goals. If the goal is to manage projects, then the most effective learning route will be through managing a project, rather than just being given theoretical knowledge about projects. When commissioning WBL, therefore, the purpose of the learning should determine the optimum mode of learning and the ideal assessment approach. Assessment is discussed in more detail in Chapter Four.

References

Armsby, P. and Costley, C. (2000) 'Research Driven Projects', in Portwood, D. and Costley, C. (2000) *Work based Learning and the University: New Perspectives and Practices*, SEDA paper 109, Birmingham

Bandura, A. (1977) *Social Learning Theory*, Prentice Hall, Englewood Cliffs, NJ

Bandura, A. (1986) *Social Foundations of Thought and Action: A Social Cognitive theory*, Prentice Hall, Englewood Cliffs, NJ

Brennan, J. and Little, B. (1996) *A Review of Work Based Learning in Higher Education*, Quality Support Centre, Department for Education and Employment, London

Brennan, J. and Little, B. (2006) *Towards a Strategy for Workplace Learning*, Centre for Higher Education Research and Information, London

CBI (2008) 'Stepping Higher: Workforce Development through employer–higher education partnership', Literature review, www.cbi.org.uk/highereducation

CBI (2009) 'Stronger Together: Businesses and universities in turbulent times', www.cbi.org.uk/highereducation

Costley, C. and Armsby, P. (2006) 'Work Based learning Assessed as a Field or a Mode of Study', *Assessment and Evaluation in Higher Education*, 31, 4, 21–33

Garnett, J. (2005) 'University Work Based Learning and the knowledge-driven project', in Rounce, K. and Workman, B. (2005) *Work-based Learning in Health Care: Applications and innovations*, Chichester, Kingsham Press

Garnett, J. (2007) 'Challenging the Structural Capital of the University to Support Work-based Learning', in Young, D. and Garnett, J. (eds) (2007) *Work-based Learning Futures*, Bolton, UVAC

Knowles, M.S., Holton III, E.F. and Answansu, R. (2005) *The Adult Learner*, 6th edition, Butterworth Heinemann, London

Nixon, I., Smith, K., Stafford, R. and Camm, S. (2006) *Work-based Learning: Illuminating the Higher Education Landscape*, The Higher Education Academy

Schön, D.A. (1987) *Educating the Reflective Practitioner. Towards a new design for Teaching and Learning in the Professions*, Jossey-Bass publishers, San Francisco

Workman, B.A. (2003) 'Methodologies in practice based projects as used by Work Based Learning students in the former School of Health, Biological and Environmental Sciences', *Journal of Health, Science and Environmental Issues*, Vol 4, 2, pp. 23–6

Table 2.1 How WBL approaches reflect a WBL continuum

	In-house training	FE/HE specifies content	Employer contributes to content	Learner negotiates content
Examples of learning activities	Demonstrations, simulations, performance skills, shadowing, social learning, training activities	Classroom/lectures, formal learning, personal reading and research, work resources, projects, learning sets, reflection	Demonstrations, simulations, shadowing, learning sets, formal and informal learning opportunities, work resources, colleagues.	Facilitated formal, informal and experiential learning, personal learning audit, personal reading and research, work resources and colleagues, reflection
Implications for job role	Specific requirements to be learned and achieved Pass/fail may have implications for job tenure	Related to job sector Pass/fail may have implications for career progression but not for current role	Related to job sector Career progression or job tenure may depend on success Learning may be constrained by organisational specific needs	Relates to individual's needs and aspirations Offers professional development and career progression Should impact upon current work role and organisational needs
Implications for delivery	On-site/close to workplace Short term programme May require some work cover during training period Needs immediate practice opportunities to consolidate training	May be taken in own time, e.g. evenings Off-site delivery, upgrades knowledge but may not relate directly to current work May need study time out, e.g. before exams/ assignments	May need training for assessors and cover while assessing learner Some delivery on-site which may impact speed of workflow Will need time out for learning, possibly role cover whilst learning and supervised practice	May be taken in own time, centres round current work activity Feeds into current work so is learning and working at the same time Some time out for reflection or further focused learning activities may be required

	In-house training	FE/HE specifies content	Employer contributes to content	Learner negotiates content
Learning support needs	Mentor/ assessor required and will need training Possibly requires access to ICT, work information and resources, intranet/ internet Supervised practice	May not have workplace assessment Education provider will give support	Mentor/assessor required and will need training Possibly requires access to ICT, work information and resources, intranet/internet Access to educational resources, e.g. library Supervised practice	Community of other practitioners or informal mentoring helpful Educational provider should give support Will need access to ICT, work information and resources, intranet/ internet and educational resources
Assessment	Prescribed by employer/ NOS, or none	Provider determines assessment May involve professional-body standards	Contributes to assessment in some form Education partner offers QA[1] framework	Assessment content and method negotiated QA of assessment provided by Education provider Degree of work involvement varies
Subject discipline	Specific for job role and competence	Builds on subject discipline related to work area, e.g. management, engineering	Specific to area of practice, supported by academic discipline, e.g. motor manufacturer supported by engineering	Specific to learners own role Cross disciplines, includes transferable skills but within culture of own subject discipline, e.g. management in health care or leadership in business, teamwork in IT

1   Quality Assurance

	In-house training	FE/HE specifies content	Employer contributes to content	Learner negotiates content
Implications for Organisation	Investment of time and resources by the organisation, links to role requirements, direct support required in the workplace	Organisation may contribute to fees or study time. New knowledge may feedback into the work role, but study may be taken without organisation's knowledge	Investment by the organisation in time, skills and resources, links to role requirements, support required from and in the workplace. Other staff development needed to facilitate further learning	Learning usually contributes directly to organisation. Negotiated learning may involve employers/community of practice or professional-body agreement. Some organisational investment may be involved through course fees, study time/conference attendance
Accreditation	May not be accredited. May have professional-body recognition	May carry accreditation ranging from Level 2 – level 7 National Qualifications Framework	May have joint accreditation between educational provider (L 2–7) and professional body	Accredited by HE. May be negotiated to evidence professional-body requirements
Outcomes	Prescribed by employer/professional body. May not have specifically articulated standards, or may use local work competences or National Occupational Standards	FE/HE determine learning outcomes/expectations, possibly with professional-body requirements. Provides QA framework for standards of achievement and processes	Employer contributes to programme outcomes and expectations. Accreditation body provides QA standards and processes	Learner determines personal learning outcomes. HE provides QA standards and processes

CHAPTER THREE

Commissioning Work Based Learning

Introduction

This chapter identifies those elements that need to be taken into account in order to choose the most appropriate commissioning approach to WBL for the organisation. It will explore the needs of the organisation and how these relate to organisational targets, and who is likely to be involved with the development and implementation of the WBL programme. The principles of commissioning for WBL will be considered together with supporting activities that are required for it to work.

Whilst there are a number of ways WBL can be undertaken, in this chapter, when discussing the commissioning process, the term 'WBL programme' has been used. This is in order to clarify that it is the whole process of identifying the learning needs, designing the approach to meeting them and evaluating the learning that is being considered, rather than a single event in the process. Whilst the process may be most effectively managed using a project approach, the term 'WBL project' has not been used as that tends to indicate a specific mode of WBL and may prove confusing.

Context

The UK economy is changing. The government agenda for developing the workforce recognises that demographic, technological and global changes in the economy will lead to different competitive pressures on all sectors and that the UK's greatest weakness in responding to these changes is the skills deficit, particularly at learning levels that reflect the midway point of a degree programme (Leitch, 2006). In particular, the UK lags behind many other countries in terms of qualifications, and a direct link is made between this deficit and future productivity as a nation. Many of the skills that have been lost are those in manufacturing and construction and, in the past, these have been associated with vocational training and learning on the job.

The workforce profile and the requirements of different roles, competences and accreditation are now also changing to accommodate this. Learning needs to be accessible, work based and available in bite-sized chunks, and recognised by flexible accreditation methods. Workforce planning, learning pathways and associated accreditation must incorporate this if learning is to have maximum impact. WBL offers an approach to learning which may help to accommodate and support these requirements, because it can be designed with the particular and current needs of the organisation in mind.

For WBL to be designed and delivered successfully, mature, facilitative partnerships between commissioners and educators need to be developed. This requires a fresh look at the skills and knowledge each can bring to the partnership, from the design and delivery of the learning through to the ongoing support for the learner, assessment methods, and accreditation.

However, workplaces need to move from the conviction that WBL is a 'good thing', just because it can happen in the workplace, to the certainty that it is an efficient, effective, and valid approach to achieve workforce development and service improvement, and one which justifies investment. All this starts with commissioning and its ultimate success depends on the robustness of that commissioning process.

Studies undertaken by the Higher Education Academy (Nixon, 2006; HEA, 2008) show that WBL can provide a cost-effective and efficient way for staff to learn in, through, and at work. Sector Skills Councils, employers, universities and other education providers are aware of the opportunities that WBL offers. However, much current WBL is conceived simply as a vehicle for individual learning, and as just another method of education and learning delivery rather than providing an opportunity for organisational development as a whole.

This is a lost opportunity. If understood as a tool for system reform or to introduce organisational change or organisation or service improvement, WBL can offer a great deal more. The best WBL emerges from the business planning process rather than being an ad-hoc and hasty solution to individual learning needs. It is led and supported within the context of consensus about the definition and delivery of WBL. It is just beginning to be understood that specifying, supporting and evaluating WBL is a complex process, and that a range of skills and attitudes are needed to contribute to this, from contracting to relationship management to evaluation. Investment is needed in the qualities, skills, and experience required by stakeholders in organisations and education providers, therefore WBL needs to be seen within the context of wider change in management processes. Clarifying the service to be delivered and the changes to be achieved are key components of the commissioning process for WBL.

Successful commissioning concerns not only the organisation and its implementation and delivery of WBL; it means thinking in advance about a whole range of components, from defining outcomes and benefits, the process(es) needed to deliver them, the staff and costs involved, as well as how it will be assessed and accredited.

The wider organisational context

In order to commission successfully, it is necessary to take into account the business plan, or the business need. Training provision is more likely to be effective if it is based on a clear understanding of the link between the aims and objectives of the organisation (e.g. customer need), with a clear rationale, and planned within a framework of overall training provision. If this is so, its **outcomes** are more easily measured later on. Increasingly, organisations have their own distinct development plan or workforce plan which is intended to support the overall desired outcomes of the business plan. The WBL programme should relate to it and be noted as such.

An example of this link can be seen in the new health-sector national workforce commissioning plan, High Quality Care For All – NHS Next Stage Review Final Report, (DoH, 2008a). It describes an intention to ensure that:

> quality is best achieved by devolving decision making to the frontline in
> an environment of transparency and clear accountabilities and where
> the role of education commissioner and education provider are clearly
> separated. We will ensure that the workforce is able to meet the needs
> of patients by developing workforce elements of service plans.... The new
> system will require leadership and management of workforce planning
> and education commissioning throughout the NHS.
>
> (DoH, 2008a: pp.73–6)

This clearly draws the needs of the business – in terms of business
outcomes, the aims of workforce planning and development and
learning/development outcomes – together. The detail of the planning
is devolved to local organisations, but within the wider framework set
out nationally. Client needs will be met through providing planned client
services. Workforce planning and development will relate to those plans.
There may be similar directives in other industrial sectors that affect
your organisation which would need to be taken into account.

So, any WBL programme needs to be planned within the context of
the wider organisational plan, and relate to its current objectives. If the
organisation has a longer-term plan, say for three or five years, it needs
to take account of those too. In the health sector example, above, a WBL
programme might be devoted to meeting specific patient needs. A local
organisation will have a more detailed strategy for how each of those
pathways will be delivered, and what that entails in practice. A WBL
programme might support that detail, or a programme might be aimed at
improving management across pathways within a particular organisation,
in which case the WBL programme would need to consider the detailed
outcomes that would be required of management, and tailor the WBL
programme accordingly.

To make sure that the detail of the commissioning plan 'fits' locally, it
should also relate to local **processes**. The organisation may have an
appraisal or personal development planning process; if so, the planned
learning should relate to this. Perhaps the organisation-wide development
plan contains some overarching principles such as the intention to
commission only learning which is competence based or mainly learning
which relates to particular qualifications or is accredited. Maybe
multidisciplinary learning is a priority. Training of differing staff grades

may be key, and therefore learning may need to be cascaded up or down the hierarchy.

Data from outside the organisation may affect the plan. For example, Skills for Health, the Sector Skills Council (SSC) for Health, has developed learning design principles around concepts that align with European level descriptors, the intention to base learning on National Occupational Standards (NOS), the need for flexible and modular provision and the intention to support skills development through the workforce (www. skillsforhealth.org.uk). A health organisation would benefit from taking these into account. It can be helpful to check out other SSC websites for this type of supporting sector information regardless of employer, since such documents do tend to determine the direction of travel for current and planned future provision. In addition, much national funding for learning is likely to be in line with them.

The more pan-organisation data collected before the learning is fully specified, the more likely it is to align with emerging best practice or wider strategic intent. At regional level, the Regional Development Agency has reports on intention regarding workforce and learning. Sector or employer-specific regional offices may have a workforce remit, with commissioning principles, or the local Learning & Skills Council or successor bodies may be worth investigating.

Commissioning as a process

The first consideration is whether to commission at all. Training and education programmes should be commissioned in response to an identified learning need. It can be assumed that training is the answer to any skills deficit or reduction of function within an organisation, and there may be other factors such as whether appropriately trained and educated individuals are in post, or whether there are organisational process issues that are restricting effective practice. Once it has been determined that staff development is the appropriate pathway, the next consideration is whether internal or external skills are required. The skills could be brought in more quickly through recruitment or staff contracts, or found in some other way, such as through reorganising existing staff more effectively. This should be weighed against the limitations that this may bring to the organisation in terms of restricting the development of the potential of the current workforce.

The learning will also need to fit within the organisation's commissioning process, if it has one. This is likely also to be related to the business plan. The Audit Commission and the former Social Services Inspectorate defined commissioning as:

> the process of specifying, securing and monitoring services to meet people's needs at a strategic level. This applies to all services whether they are provided by the local authority, other public agencies and the private or voluntary sectors.

(Audit commission website)

Commissioning can take place on three levels: strategic (defining overall services and context); operational (procuring and monitoring those services); and individual (packages of services for individuals within the plan). Commissioning strategies are often underpinned by a set of guiding *principles* or overall intentions. For example, those of the audit commission include:

- Plan and consult
- Value for money
- Sustainable procurement
- Developing and valuing our people
- Knowledge and information
- Excellence (see Audit Commission website/procurement).

The health sector recently developed a comprehensive commissioning strategy – 'World Class Commissioning' (DoH, 2008b). It aims to deliver a more strategic and long-term approach to commissioning services, with a clear focus on delivering improved health outcomes. There are four key elements to the programme: a vision for world-class commissioning, a set of world-class commissioning competencies, an assurance system and a support and development framework. In the absence of a similar programme in other industrial sectors, these key elements could be amended to assist in determining appropriate commissioning processes.

WBL is an investment in the business and therefore the following factors should be considered:

- The impact on delivering contracts
- The effect on outcomes for clients
- The impact on recruitment and retention
- The demand of the market
- The emerging organisation commissioning priorities.

Financial costs are discussed below, but a cost benefit analysis may be necessary if the planned WBL is large scale or if there is doubt about the value of commissioning it. The Kirkpatrick model of evaluation (Kirkpatrick, 1994), which will be outlined in the evaluation chapter, has some useful checklists to aid cost prediction for learning and development.

What is the purpose of the WBL programme?

Once there is certainty about the relationship between the proposed project and the wider aims of the organisation, planning the WBL programme can start. The following questions can act as an initial checklist to develop clarity about the aims of the programme.

Why does the learning need to take place?

This question is often the easiest to answer, as most people find it fairly simple to describe the immediate learning need. It is a useful starting point for identifying the learning need more clearly. However, the initial answer to this question is often amended in the light of the answers to the other questions considered below. An identified learning need may arise from a number of sources – an individual member of staff may define it, or it may come from another source, such as a team or a manager from the same department or elsewhere. It may even be suggested or demanded by a customer or business partner. It is worth querying whether the problem can really be solved through learning or whether it is an organisational issue which can be solved in some other way.

The following questions will help to define the learning need:

- What difference will the learning make to customers or clients?

Identifying what is expected as an outcome will make it easier to measure success later.

- What outcomes does the organisation need to achieve?

What does the organisation or department need specifically from the learning? What will be different as a result?

- What are the short-, medium- and long-term benefits to the organisation of the planned learning?

What measurable benefits are envisaged from the learning?

- How does this align with the organisation's development plan?
- If there is wider development or learning taking place in the organisation, how does this project relate to it?
- What sort of WBL approach would be best?

In what ways would a WBL approach be best? How much of the learning can be supported in-house?

- What would be the costs to the organisation if this learning were not commissioned?

Are there risks or costs associated with not commissioning this work? How important are these?

- Will the changes justify the costs to the organisation?

Are the benefits of the development likely to outweigh the costs of procuring and supporting them?

At this point the plan is likely to be in early draft stage and might not even be written down. Asking these questions at this juncture, before the real planning of the project takes places, makes it less likely that a great deal of work will be undertaken and come to nothing. If it is clear at this stage that there is real doubt about the costs versus the benefits then the project will not be cost effective. If the outcomes from the learning can be simply and cheaply supplied locally, then an external WBL programme may not be the best approach, but ways to achieve the learning internally will still need to be addressed. However, if the project seems to be viable at this stage then more detailed planning is required. This is explored in depth in the next chapter.

Costs

Learning, like any other service, needs to be cost effective. Certainty about the investment will require some estimation of the resources the learning is likely to require, and the cost or value of those resources to the organisation. For example, costs should take into account:

- Staff 'time out' for learning, and the possible need to cover positions

- Potential disruption to service delivery if staff are learning on or off site

- Staff time assigned to mentoring or coaching learners at work

- Costs of any additional equipment or learning materials

- Whether roles and functions may change as a result of the learning

- And if so, whether there will be costs associated with any services, systems or job roles which will need to be redesigned.

There is also the possibility of non-achievement by some of the learners, which has implications for both the workforce and the individual. The impact of this on the overall plan, the staff and the workplace will need to be considered and, where possible, plans put in place to ameliorate it. Failure in the workplace, where previously someone has been able to function, can have a negative effect on some workers. Those whose educational experience was negative and who dislike formal learning may resist additional learning or education and that may have an impact on the rest of a department.

Additionally, the investment of time required to build partnerships with organisations and people involved, and to deliver successful WBL jointly should be factored in. This investment is crucial, because the better providers of learning and their client organisations understand each other, the better the learning is planned, and the more successful the outcomes.

Setting up and maintaining an effective partnership to ensure learning occurs and is absorbed into the workplace is an essential factor of success. Partnership working is considered in Chapter Four. Moreover, the budget may need to accommodate changes, compromises or extensions to the original plan so it is good to build in some flexibility if possible.

By now, it should be possible to arrive at a reasonable idea of some of the cost justifications which will need to be considered and their implications. Some people may find it useful to draw up a checklist of these, using a form similar to the one below. All 'hidden' costs should be included.

Here are a few examples of how costs might be affected:

Evidence indicates that the costs of this learning are justified because:	costs
We will lose x business unless we train	
Clients relations will be improved by x	
We will improve staff flexibility for the future because...	
These skills are difficult to recruit. We know because...	
The amount of time we will save if staff can do this directly has been quantified at x	
Mentor training, time out and back fill to cover roles will cost x	

Value for money

Getting value for money can be complex. Certainly, the National Audit Office (NAO) expects value for money where the organisation commissioning is using public funds. The NAO defines value for money in relation to three areas:

Economy – minimising the cost of resources used

Efficiency – the relationship between the output from goods or services and the resources used to produce them

Effectiveness – the relationship between the intended and actual results of the public spending.

Now review the overall reasons driving the WBL initiative. These may be about, for example, seeking to improve turnover or increasing profit. For some, the aim might be to improve customer retention rates or satisfaction or be designed to provide new services for clients by developing staff members who currently do not have the right skills.

To determine the answers to all these, stakeholders – such as line managers or supervisors or others directly concerned with the service provided – should be consulted. The use of SMART targets will help to refine some outcome indicators and outcome measures. These five principles will identify outcome indicators and outcome measures, and focus on what is to be captured and how to record it:

SMART Targets

Specific
- Well defined
- Clear to others

Measurable
- Know if the goal is obtainable and how far away completion is
- Know when it has been achieved

These specific markers will be recorded to monitor progress and success

Achievable
- Doable, able to be achieved
- Agreement with all stakeholders about goals

Realistic
- Within the availability of resources, knowledge and time

Timely
- Enough time to achieve the goal
- Undertaken within an appropriate time frame

Once a plan has been developed it may need some adjustment in terms of what is possible locally and within a national context. The regional strategic development plan produced by the Regional Development Agency might be useful in order to help highlight local labour-market considerations. Locally identified skill needs and shortages will also be considered here, as well as from other sources. Key information about government funding opportunities to upskill local workforces may be available through these routes and may assist the organisation in making an investment decision. Having taken these external and internal factors into account, and consequently refined the plan, other people who may be able to contribute can be identified and involved. This will ensure that the final plan is robust.

Timeliness can be a real consideration. The time frame within which the learning needs to happen should be considered, taking into account the impact on staff, clients and any other agencies or organisations involved. For example, delivery time should be considered, since programmes that need to be run in conjunction with FE or HE institutions may need to fit into the academic calendar, and this may have implications for when worker–learners are able to attend programmes.

For example, the retail trade would not want to release staff at peak sales times such as Christmas or January, and sports clubs may not want to lose staff during the peak competitive summer months. The programme's fit with the organisation's time patterns is therefore important.

Release of funds in relation to the beginning and end of financial years, whether that is the year end or the tax year may limit when WBL programmes can be paid for and consequently when programmes can be delivered.

There may be wider issues to consider such as the impact of the planned learning on standards of service delivery, or whether it conflicts with the timescales of any wider organisational development activity. It has happened that some planned large learning projects have been shelved or abandoned because it was later discovered that an organisation or regional funding review was working to a different timescale or because the learning needed to fit with a project led by other staff in the organisation. There may be some unfortunate cost implications to this, which could be avoided. Funds can be channelled more appropriately if the timing is considered strategically.

An additional key issue when determining value for money whilst contracting is to take into account that the cheapest option is not always the best value. Value for money is equally about making sure that the work which is agreed is the best fit for the purpose, and can be as much about confidence that the organisation commissioned has the right skills and experience for the work. Failure to get this right can lead to poor value outcomes, and can also waste costly time in managing and rectifying mistakes at a later date, so careful pre-planning based on required outcomes is essential.

Practicalities to be factored in

Another way of thinking about value for money in terms of WBL may be in relation to macro and micro values and measures. Macro issues affecting cost might include:

- Whether there is potential for learners to acquire credits

- Probable changes in practice as a result of the learning

- Improvement in recruitment and retention

- Improvement in staff morale

- Improvement in services received by people

- Improved outcomes for people receiving services

- Service delivery influenced by specific work-based learning

- Impact on other organisational activities.

A public-sector organisation commissioner might wish to consider the potential to respond to new litigation, local authority targets or other performance standards and targets. In the private sector, first considerations may be whether the outcomes will have the potential to contribute towards measurable efficiency savings and related targets.

Micro issues might be more immediate and project specific. For example:

- Costs of equipment

- Costs of travel

- Time lost from work
- Costs of assessor or organisation staff time
- Costs of replacing staff absent from work for offsite learning
- Alternative cost-effective ways of acquiring this skill base.

Here are some examples of potential benefits of WBL, which were identified for the health sector:

For clients:
- *changes in practice*
- *improved outcomes or products for clients*
- *improvements in service delivery and/or quality*
- *improvements in output/activity*

For learners:
- *acquiring skills, knowledge and experience*
- *acquiring credits and qualifications*
- *career development*
- *professional recognition and/or academic reward*
- *improvement in morale*
- *greater job satisfaction*
- *greater productivity*
- *reduction in sickness/absence*
- *acknowledgement of capability or role potential*
- *contribution to the organisational knowledge and personal intellectual capital*

For the organisation:

- *achieving the organisation's development priorities*
- *improvement in recruitment and retention*
- *improved service governance and risk management*
- *adherence to quality and service standards*
- *implementation of evidence-based practice*
- *improved viability in the market place*
- *capturing organisational knowledge*
- *improved position in the market sector*
- *improved staff capability and therefore potential to respond to future pressures*
- *development of organisation's human, intellectual and structural capital*

Summary

By this stage in the commissioning process, the key steps involved should be clear. A business case to the organisation for why the learning is necessary can be made, and the key people who can help should be apparent. High-level expectations for the learning, expected outcomes, and some early thoughts about success measures should also be evident. An idea of what it will cost, whether it is worth the investment, and how it will be sponsored should be emerging too.

All of this early planning is certainly the most important work of the whole project and will repay the effort expended. Data will have been captured which can be used later. In the next chapter the development of this plan will be explored in more detail; but before progressing to it, review the following questions to ensure that the key facts for your organisation have been gathered.

Commissioning specification – checklist of components

A commissioning specification can be devised which can lead to useful preparatory discussions to negotiate all that is required. The following checklist may help:

- Is the main rationale for the programme clear? What are the key drivers for this? These will sustain it through the challenges of getting it up and running.

- Is there clarity about how the proposed programme fits within, and supports, the wider business of the organisation?

- Is there clarity about how the proposed programme relates to and supports any strategic training principles, such as using a competence-based approach?

- Is there clarity about any links between the proposed programme and any other current, recent or proposed training or development initiatives?

- Have the organisational outcomes been identified – the expected impact of the learning on the business, and any associated measures (in outline)?

- Have the key organisation(s) and people involved been identified?

- Has anyone identified the overall project budget available, and can the costs of the project versus the benefits to the business be identified?

- Has the most appropriate size of the learning cohort been considered in relation to issues of viability, tutorial support and time, time out for study and any replacement staffing costs?

- Have the organisational leads been identified and has consideration been given to their key responsibilities? Leadership and coordination are crucial roles and need to be specific at outset: who will lead and who has the authority to commission and agree terms and responsibilities?

- Have the scale of the project and its time frame been specified?

- Have the group(s) of learners been targeted – by service, team or department as appropriate?

- Has consideration been given to whether vocational recognition or academic credit would be appropriate for the learning? (See Chapter Four for more detail on this issue.)

- Will commissioning an external provider be the best solution and, if so, will this fit within the organisation's commissioning protocols? If not, has an internal provider been identified?

References

Audit Commission website, http://www.audit-commission.gov.uk/localgov/pages/default.aspx, accessed March 2010

Caley, L. (2006) *Learning for Health Improvement: A Practical Guide for the Workplace*, Radcliffe Publishing

DoH (2008a) 'High Quality Care for All', NHS Next Stage review Final Report, London, June 2008 http://www.dh.gov.uk/dr_consum_dh/groups/dh_digitalassets/@dh/@en/documents/digitalasset/dh_085828.pdf

DoH (2008b) 'World Class Commissioning', www.dh.gov.uk/en/managing_yourorganisation/commissioning/worldclasscommissioning/index.htm

Hardacre, K. and Masterson, K. (2007) *Typology of Assessment Methods*, June 2007, www.skillsforhealth.org.uk/uploads/page/89/uploadablefile.pdf

HEA (2008) *Work-based Learning Costing Study*, HEA, York

Kirkpatrick, D.L. (1994) *Evaluating Training Programmes: the four levels*, Berrett-Koehler

Leitch, S. (2006) *Prosperity for all in the global economy – world class skills*, HMSO, Norwich

Nixon, I. (2006) *Work based learning: Illuminating the Higher Education Landscape*, Higher Education Academy

Pulliam Phillips, P. and Phillips, J.J. (2005) *Return on Investment*, (ROI) Basics, ASTD Press

Useful Websites

www.businessballs.com – useful summaries and forms on a number of learning issues e.g. costings.

www.learnatwork.info – Socrates Minerva project (2005–8) focusing on the use of ICT to enhance the induction and continuing support for learners in the workplace.

www.mdx.ac.uk/wbl – Partnerships – Institute for Work Based Learning, Middlesex University

http://www.nao.org.uk/what_we_do/value_for_money_audit.aspx

http://www.skillsforhealth.org.uk – Skills for Health Learning Design Principles

CHAPTER FOUR

Developing a plan

Guidance for developing the case for the WBL programme has been presented and initial thought given to the rationale for the development and what it would aim to achieve. It has been suggested that the financial outlay would pay off if certain factors were considered as part of the preparation. At this stage, a more detailed plan can be developed. This chapter will explore the development of the WBL programme particularly in the area of working with stakeholders.

Determining appropriate outcome indicators and evidence for the impact of WBL is considered and some practical questions for commissioners and line managers are included to help guide the development plan. Accreditation of learning and the different forms that recognising learning can take are also discussed.

Defining key stakeholders

Stakeholders are those people and organisations who may affect, be affected by, or perceive themselves to be affected by, a decision or activity. In the case of WBL, the stakeholders are key partners in determining why and what learning needs to take place. They are often in the best position to define the business or service need and they are likely to be of great help. They can help to:

- Define and make clear the learning outcomes required

- Create specific indicators or measures of whether these outcomes have been achieved

- Support or mentor learners

- Provide specific learning opportunities

- Assess learners

- Support evaluation.

If the WBL programme is especially complex, a steering or advisory group, and perhaps subgroups of it, may need to be organised. If so, these key stakeholders are the people most likely to be useful members of such groups:

- Learners

- Line managers

- Practice facilitators

- Service users/clients/customers

- Carers/supporters

- Co-workers

- Staff in other relevant departments, depending on the aims of the learning

- External commissioners

- External or internal providers of the learning/training

- Mentors

- Supervisors.

Depending on the type and level of influence of staff undertaking the WBL, and the nature of the WBL itself, other stakeholders could be added to this list. Each team will wish to consider the stakeholders with whom it needs to consult.

Designers and evaluators of WBL may consider stakeholders in terms of importance, or influential power interest. This can help ensure that the right stakeholders are involved, and it is important to do this before any learning is commissioned. In defining stakeholders and determining their role, it can be helpful to ask what the effect on the success of the project would be if each person/organisation were not consulted in any way.

The following two examples make a good case for employing the stakeholder model.

Example 1

We have just completed a programme of work-based learning commissioned from our local university, which was aimed at improving the business planning skills of our project managers. We started by identifying line managers and others affected by their skills in this area. In the end we included the finance team, the organisation's lead business development manager and a couple of line managers of the staff concerned. We included a member of the university staff, the HR department commissioning the learning and finally a client on whose behalf the project managers work.

All of these people were able to help us with the project. It would have been very tricky to come up with concrete, measurable ways in which we could determine whether the outcomes of the project were contributing to better organisational practice unless the finance and business development managers had offered to contribute a list of success measures and timeframes for them. The university was pleased that line managers were so involved as they have had problems coordinating the university learning with work-based practice and experience. Our line managers came up with ways of offering these opportunities that only they could have thought of, as they fell naturally out of the work going on in their teams.

In the end, cost projections and timescale management were improved for our clients and provably so. Everyone was able to measure and see that this saved time, and therefore money, as well as clients' tempers!

Construction company manager

Example 2

Last year we undertook a learning programme across the medical directorate, involving four wards. We included blended learning and a range of development opportunities for staff. We thought we had checked that what we had planned and delivered was what was needed. However, when we came to review at the end, we discovered that the ward managers had a different view from us about the success of the initiative, and didn't feel that all needs had been met. We realise now that if we had identified and prioritised our stakeholders, and mapped the expected outcomes and taken care to agree them with all, we would have a better outcome.

NHS Trust HR Department

What outcomes does the organisation need to achieve?

Real clarity is required regarding expected outcomes in order to achieve effective WBL. This is a lot of work, but it will pay off later. Breaking down the outcomes required for each different group affected, and including the outcomes required for the organisation, the service or team, for the learners, and for clients will make them specific and achievable. By spending some time trying to distinguish between these outcomes, each participant's expectations will become much clearer. However, taken as a whole, it should offer a broad overview to both the organisation and education provider of what is required, and of whom. Involving stakeholders will really help with this work.

This exercise can also reveal where outcomes can conflict or overlap, and where action can be taken to resolve this. For example, line managers may be looking for simple skill development whereas department managers may hope the learning will help to deliver a particular strategy, but for everyone in the department it might change the context in which the learning is delivered.

The term 'outcomes' is used here to mean **the positive changes, benefits, learning or other effects** that are expected to result from WBL.

An outcomes-focused approach to commissioning WBL involves:

- Identifying the changes required

- Checking the list of changes expected by all the stakeholders involved

- Commissioning and delivery of the programme

- Capturing information and data to help understand the changes that take place

- Using the findings to inform and redesign (or re-commission) development opportunities in order to achieve required changes.

Consequently, identification and capturing of outcome indicators and measures should be considered.

Outcome indicators are those changes which may be *indirectly* attributed to an action or intervention. For example, if a change in practice is implemented through WBL, and customers give positive feedback about the change in practice, then their feedback may be considered to be an outcome *indicator*. A line manager's view that a team performs better after training, if not backed up with hard data, is an indicator.

Outcome measures are those changes which are attributed to an action or intervention, *and which are measurable.* The line manager in the example above may show data which measures the change in staff after the learning, such as increased volume in work activity or outputs. For example, if within a hospital unit additional staff members are trained as phlebotomists, resulting in an increase in blood tests being undertaken within the unit within a set period, then the increased number of blood tests within this period may be considered an outcome *measure*. Equally, in a retail environment, if improved development for staff coincides with an increase in sales, this increase in sales can be measured and may be attributed to the development. Having clarity about both outcome measures and outcome indicators will be enormously helpful when evaluating the WBL later.

An example outcome: making a difference to customers or clients

The predicted outcomes of the WBL to be commissioned will include the difference it makes to customers and clients. It is expected that the outcomes of most programmes will make a difference to people in the organisation, in terms of the way they work, but the key outcomes are likely to be required for the organisation itself.

Specifically predicting these outcomes and giving some advance thought to how they might be measured will be useful. So, if it is hoped that some learning will change the way a service is provided or managed in order to raise the number of sales for a department, then the questions needing further thought might be:

- By what percentage might sales rise?

- How will this be measured?

- Who will collect the information?

- Over what period might the measurement take place?

- Can these outcomes be attributed to other factors not connected with the learning programme?

Care should be taken with these last two issues. There will be a time delay before expected outcomes are likely to take effect. Also, there can be occasions where it is impossible to state with any certainty (objectively) that the reasons a business need was met were directly a result of the learning taking place. Subjectively, however, anecdotal evidence from stakeholders can be invaluable at a fairly early stage in giving a feel for whether the learning is making or has made a difference.

Trying to clarify how learning is intended to make a difference to the objectives of the business is important, as it helps to focus those involved in the process and support the rationale for the investment in the first place, as well as providing evidence towards the business case for learning in the organisation.

Key practical questions for commissioners

You should now know the aims of the WBL and what is to be achieved from it. This is the starting point. However, there are a few additional issues worth considering. If commissioning the WBL, additional questions to ask might be:

- *Is this learning happening elsewhere? If so, what can we take from it?*

There is usually plenty of evidence about good practice or lessons which others have learned on the Web, and elsewhere. Even a brief perusal of this may reveal some information about what to do, or what to avoid.

- *Can the learning be purchased 'off the shelf' (and adapted if necessary), or does it need to be designed specifically for this purpose?*

If others elsewhere have carried out this particular piece of work, or something fairly near to it, this may enable a fast track to a suitable programme.

- *What timescales are we working to, and what does that tell us about the type of programme that can be commissioned?*

Since timescale constraints and learners' availability will inevitably influence what can be achieved, it is worth bearing this in mind at the start.

- *Should the learning be aligned with regulatory requirements? Can we take the opportunity to meet other targets through the learning? e.g. professional-body targets or those of industry regulators.*

A number of professional bodies develop standards of their own, and also link standards with the requirements of any industry regulators. It is worth considering whether they may add value – previously in some sectors they have been written and organised differently to national occupational standards, which has caused confusion for commissioners and designers. Professional-body standards, such as are found in the management sector, may also inform a programme.

- *Can National Occupational Standards (NOS), or parts of NOS, help to define my requirements?*

Increasingly, a competence framework is used in order to define standards (performance criteria) and levels for units (or amounts) of learning. Accessing these allows for a shared language for learning by all involved. It also makes it easier to discover whether and how this learning has been undertaken elsewhere, since the same unit titles are carried across qualifications.

Traditionally universities have not been involved in the competence movement, although the further education sector has. However, this is changing, as Sector Skills Councils promote their use. Competences may be available at higher-education level, or organisational competences may be designed specifically to meet organisational objectives and consequently be incorporated into development.

- *Does the learning need to be transferable?*

If it does, this strengthens the case for, at least, linking the work with national occupational standards, industry competences and the Qualifications and Credit Framework (QCF) (www.qcda.gov.uk). Government has argued strongly for ensuring that learning is capable of being used elsewhere, partly because of the wastage involved in replicating learning in different contexts and 'languages'. A response to the question of "has anyone else already done this?" can be to visit the QCDA website to find out. The QCF is a new framework for recognising and accrediting qualifications in England, Wales and Northern Ireland. The framework is central to a major reform of the vocational qualifications system and is designed to simplify the system and be easier to use. The aim is to make the qualifications and the system for recording them more relevant to the needs of employers and more flexible and accessible for learners. However, it does not necessarily include a full range of higher-education opportunities, and it would be appropriate to contact the local HE institution to discuss organisational requirements.

Key practical questions for line managers

Line managers and others more directly associated with supporting the learning process may want to consider some additional issues.

- *Is the learning linked with the organisation's appraisal processes?*

If this is considered at the design stage, existing appraisal and performance management structures might be able to be used to support the learning. This saves time on duplication of processes, and also ensures that the learning connects to the needs of teams. It can also be used as a mechanism to record learning needs and completions, and whether the learning was appropriate for the individual's learning needs.

- *Are the learning objectives aligned with the expectations of the team and the learner(s)?*

This should not be a problem if the stakeholder model previously outlined is employed, as views of stakeholders can be taken into account, and any emerging difference of opinion resolved at an early stage.

- *Is the learning achievable, given staffing and business/service priorities? Can staff be released for study or development, when necessary?*

If there are doubts here, can anything else be done at this stage to avoid duplication of existing effort? Can the learning be linked to other initiatives or partly delivered using the organisation's existing team processes? There are likely to be at least some opportunities within the organisation to enhance learning 'on the job'. Any problems which can be foreseen and addressed here will help to speed up the learning process and avoid disappointment or learner dropout later, which wastes resources.

- *Are any of the skills required to assess/contribute to the assessment of learners in the team in place?*

Many staff and supervisors may already be skilled in and contributing to other assessment activities, particularly in the public sector. Taking this into account will ensure that staff are not overburdened with mentoring and assessment tasks, but also that unused assessment skills are engaged. Introducing WBL can offer staff development opportunities for experienced staff through learning mentoring and assessment skills. Assessment is considered further in Chapter Five.

One commissioner comments:

> We found that the obstacles to delivering work-based learning can be overcome as long as staff really believed that the learning will help to ease pressures of delivery. Effective preparation of staff and managers, as well as clearly identified service need, is key to achieving this.

NHS manager

What sort of WBL approach would be best?

Before anything changes, what suggests that WBL is the best approach? This question should be answerable from the scoping work that has been done so far.

The different types of WBL that could be used were outlined in Chapter Two, but it will be important that the organisation and the provider have discussed the best approach that meets both their expectations. WBL is not necessarily the cheapest approach as time for learning will have to be factored in, as will supervision of new skills, and additional learning for supervisors or assessors may need to be considered. Therefore the type of WBL that will be used must be agreed upon at an early stage. Additional questions to consider are:

- Will it include further education or higher education links or accreditation?

- Will National Occupational Standards or those from professional bodies be used as benchmarks?

- If so, will that incur additional costs? If so, is there funding available from the Sector Skills Councils, Local Authority, European Union or Regional Development Agency grants or similar?

These factors may depend heavily on local needs such as employment rates and regeneration initiatives.

Partnership with education providers

If an education provider is commissioned, a partnership approach is crucial to delivering the best result. The WBL needs to be shaped and supported by a partnership between the employer commissioning the learning, the organisation supporting the learning, the provider delivering the learning, and the learners themselves.

Often, commissioners and providers are insufficiently clear about their own responsibilities and consequently the responsibility and role of the others involved. The education provider is likely to have a fair amount of experience from previous programmes about what can work best, and what resources are likely to be required of the commissioning organisation. Getting to know providers well, and having an effective strategy for working and communicating with them, is likely to lead to creative insights on both sides about what can be achieved. For example, commissioners of WBL, or the organisations they represent, may be in a better position to contribute in-house teaching to staff about the use of some up-to-date procedures, skills and technologies, whereas education providers may be better placed to support and manage other elements, such as organisation of learning, including the mode of delivery and accreditation. Scrutinising what each party offers, and asking questions about the how, where, when and what of the programme and the expectations that are inherent within it, will provide the opportunity to determine roles and responsibilities of each party. Those with previous experience, such as the educational provider, may well have specific requirements within a memorandum of co-operation which makes these factors explicit.

Getting to the bottom of these kinds of insights requires spending time exploring beneath the 'headlines' of the possible contract.

Some areas to consider when planning a partnership with a WBL provider are:

- Relative responsibilities and expectations of the employer, their learners and the education provider

- The degree of commitment from participating organisations, such as time period

- Level of commitment and support needed from each party such as who will track the learners' progress

- Whether the organisation or the provider will provide tutorial or additional support time

- Whether the provider will share information about the learners' success or failure and who has permission to access it

- Who will monitor attendance

- Whether the organisation will guarantee release from work, and/or additional study time

- Assessment responsibilities and expectations, particularly if practice assessment is required.

Accreditation

The nature of accreditation

Accreditation of learning refers to academic or vocational accreditation conferred on learners by learning providers and their regulators. It recognises learning achievement in the form of an academic level, relating to the difficulty and amount of study. This accounts for the value of the award, usually in the form of credits, either in hours of study, or points on an award scale. For example, accreditation by FE (Further Education) usually equates to GCSE and A level standards, even if the type of award is in a different form, such as NVQs, Business and Technology Education Consortium (BTEC) or Open College Network (OCN) awards. Accreditation by HE reflects university-level learning and therefore equates with programmes being run within the university, either in academic level or content. This accreditation is distinct from that of professional bodies which takes place between professional bodies and vocational or academic providers. Academic accreditation cannot be awarded for learning that is not assessed and this also differentiates academic from professional accreditation.

Accreditation is different from validation because the process of the learning usually takes place outside the accrediting institution and may have been originally designed to meet non-academic objectives (Challis and Raban, 1999). Accreditation differs from assessment, as it recognises and ascribes a value to learning, or components or modules of learning, and gives it a form of transferable currency whereas assessment determines whether individual learners have achieved the learning outcomes and standards of their programme of study.

As with any other form of HE provision, accreditation of WBL has to take place within the quality assurance infrastructure of either vocational or higher education quality standards. The quality assurance process of an assessed learning activity enables the learning from the workplace to be recognised as valid within a university setting, but tailored to the requirements of an organisation (Graham, Helyer and Workman, 2008). WBL accreditation challenges HE because it involves recognition of learning that occurs in the workplace, rather than in HE, and for some academics this raises issues regarding the validity of the knowledge that is generated from work practices.

Accreditation of WBL may be perceived to be expensive for HE in comparison to more taught courses as it is more personalised. However, it can greatly improve the relationships between universities and employers through collaboration, and through each gaining an understanding of the others' issues. It has been noted that universities benefit from accrediting organisations as this ensures HE staff maintain currency with work practices in different sectors and also provides opportunities for organisational development work (Rounce, 2005). For some employers this is highly significant as the sheer speed of technological advance in the workplace can mean that high-level skills are more likely to be found in workplaces than with traditional education providers, and so new university graduates require further skills to become ready for the workplace.

The Quality Assurance Agency for higher education has published a code of practice for work-based and placement learning, which can be found at www.qaa.ac.uk/academicinfrastructure/codeofpractice/section9/. This has been used to give advice on learning in the workplace from the perspective of HE, but also identifies what the accompanying responsibilities could be for employers. Additionally, the South East Education Consortium (SEEC) has produced *Notes for Guidance for Work-related Learning*. The notes contain a set of eight precepts with accompanying guidance on arrangements for work-related learning. These notes meet the required standard for quality assurance in HE, while accommodating the practical operational issues in running work-related learning programmes.

Why accredit?

Until fairly recently, much WBL has been informal, in that it was designed in-house to meet immediate need, or not subject to the rigours of academic oversight in any way, regardless of its quality. Increasingly, employers are seeing the benefit of getting accreditation for WBL, in order to 'kitemark' it, and acknowledge that the quality of the learning is as high as external education provision. Learners often like accredited learning, partly for the quality assurance, but more so because they can gain a certificate for their learning which is transferable when they move jobs, and which recognises the learning they have achieved. It can be particularly heartening for learners in lower-level vocational programmes to realise that the learning they have undertaken in their jobs is 'worth' a qualification, as they may have previously experienced difficulty in their formal education experience, and find it particularly motivating to receive recognition of their learning.

For employers, accredited learning not only provides an external benchmark for their development and a career progression route for staff, but it motivates staff and recognises the value of the work and learning that they are involved in. Recognising and capturing the learning from work improves performance and shares knowledge between colleagues, thereby keeping knowledge in the organisation to inform future practice

(Graham, Helyer and Workman, 2008). It also provides a vehicle for ensuring that work-based and external learning is not duplicated, and therefore saves on development funds. Accredited learning can act as an indicator for any national or regional quality standards or initiatives with which the organisation is involved, such as Investors in People.

Should accreditation be appropriate, the educational provider will work with the organisation to prepare appropriate documentation and evidence in order to assess the level and amount of learning. The route that learners can take with their accredited learning may be circumscribed by the accreditation process – for example, as part of a Foundation degree or towards a particular college award – but it is important to consider progression possibilities as part of the accreditation plan.

Assessment of learning

Assessment is a critical but complex dimension of WBL. It can be designed to capture both long- and short-term outcomes, and offers an opportunity for creative partnerships with learning providers. It is often managed and coordinated by education providers, with particular assessment responsibilities (such as practice assessment or mentoring support and feedback in the assessment process) delegated to the learners' organisation.

The best assessment is flexible. It calls on a wide range of success criteria in order to capture outcomes and changes. Assessment needs to be designed carefully at the outset, in order to ensure clarity between education providers and commissioners regarding the responsibility for developing and/or providing assessment. The potential burden of assessment on organisations needs to be taken into account, with a view to keeping assessment as simple and as reliable as possible. Finally, it needs to make best use of the work environment. Ideally it should be related to the desired outcomes of the WBL. If additional development or education has been undertaken in line with organisational objectives, then it makes sense to design practical assessment that demonstrates achievement of those objectives. For HE assessment, there is usually a written component in order to demonstrate achievement against HE-level criteria. It may be accompanied by a variety of methods of evidence that demonstrates learning has been acquired, such as digital video, portfolios or the production of artefacts such as information leaflets. Various forms of suitable assessment strategies are explored in more detail in the next chapter.

Assessment for accreditation needs to be as rigorous as the assessment of learning that takes place in education, with similar assurance of quality, even though assessors may not be university staff, particularly as what is assessed may be outside the scope of the traditional university subject-based curriculum. Usually the assessment activities are designed as part of the accreditation process to ensure that they are commensurate with formal learning processes.

The main questions regarding assessment that all WBL programmes have to address are:

- Who is responsible for developing the assessment strategy?

- How will the context of the assessment, i.e. at work, influence the assessment method?

- How will it be developed?

- What resources can be made available for assessment within the organisation?

- Can a dedicated member of staff coordinate assessment?

- Is there room for joint assessment with other initiatives, to save resources?

- What skills will the assessors need to have, and are they already in place?

- Who will do the assessment?

It is important to note that staff with direct line-management responsibility for the worker–learners should not also assess them, although they may contribute to assessment managed by others.

Each sector and industry will have its own checklist of indicators against which assessment needs to be judged. Here is a detailed one from the health sector which is currently struggling to resolve complex assessment issues related to practice and fitness for purpose. Some of the criteria here are relevant everywhere – for example, assessment should always be fair – but some may seem less relevant to other sectors. In this example, the benefit of linking with a national knowledge and skills framework specific to health is apparent. This is the case because the health sector is particularly concerned to address problems associated with joining up a plethora of existing assessment frameworks and activities which can make assessment generally burdensome for health staff.

Below is a checklist produced by the health sector to outline the optimal requirements of assessment. The checklist pulls together all of the things which would be in place if assessment processes were running at an optimum level. Many of the statements are likely to apply to other organisations and, in large and complex organisations, most of them would be relevant.

Optimal assessment – health sector

- Capable of aligning assessment provision, where possible, across the vocational and academic divide and between professional groups

- Managed within an effective quality assurance system, and includes effective standardisation

- Valid, reliable, sufficient and authentic

- Appropriate and proportionate to the decision made (both in terms of level and the evidence)

- Undertaken by those alongside whom the learner works

- Timely, and involves ongoing and continuous elements as necessary

- Capable of acknowledging and reflecting existing competence (including accrediting learning and skills already held) and able to lend itself to developmental (formative) learning where necessary

- Appropriate in terms of methods used

- Well planned by the assessor

- Transferable and consistent in terms of results

- Inclusive of opportunities for effective and high-quality feedback

- Consistent and joined up with broader HR strategy, e.g. the Knowledge and Skills Framework (KSF), or other developmental systems in place locally

- Cost and time effective

- Adaptable for a range of needs, including staff groups and type of qualification

- Proportionate to the risk to clients, scope of roles and staff level, and regulation requirements

- Linked to identified workforce planning needs, which are based on some national or area level workforce planning principles or information

- Capable of being planned in a clear, concise and jargon-free way.

Hardacre and Masterson (2007)

Key activities for detailed planning are summarised in the following checklist:

Checklist – Developing a plan

Overall

- Identify stakeholders and the approach which will be used to work with them

- Define the detailed learning objectives for all, including learner–workers, trainers and educators

- Develop outcome indicators and measures in order to be able to measure long-term performance

- Clearly define the infrastructure, resources and organisational responsibilities required to ensure delivery

- Determine how the organisation will expect the learners to apply new knowledge and skills in the workplace and what could happen to the job role if they do not or cannot

- Consider monitoring and governance arrangements, including milestones, and identify who is responsible for the time-consuming role of partnership approaches and managing expectations.

Technical

- Determine how issues of transferability and portability of learning will be handled, and whether accreditation of portable or more tailored qualifications is desirable

- If credits towards a larger qualification are desirable, how can that progression be factored into the commissioning?

- Clarify WBL approaches to be used, including the key characteristics and structure of the WBL (e.g. short courses, once only, versus long courses and university awards)

- Consider workload and time commitments expected of the learners and assessors.

References

Challis, M. and Raban, C. (1999) *Higher Education: Learning from Experience?* Sheffield Hallam University Press, Sheffield

Graham, S., Helyer, R. and Workman, B. (2008) 'Accreditation of in-company training provision: an overview of models and issues', in *Work-based Learning, Workforce development: Connections, frameworks and processes*, HEA, York, www.heacademy.ac.uk

Hardacre, K. and Masterson, A. (2007) *Exploring best practice in the assessment of competence in the health sector*, available from Skills for Health

Rounce, K. (2005) 'Organisational Accreditation: experience in the health sector', in Rounce, K. and Workman, B. (2005) *Work Based Learning in Health Care: Applications and Innovations*, Kingsham press, Chichester

South East Education Consortium (SEEC), *Notes for Guidance for Work-related Learning*, available from the publications list of the website: www.seec.org.uk

CHAPTER FIVE

Building the capacity to deliver the WBL plan

Most of the preparatory work has now been carried out. Stakeholders have been identified, as have detailed project outcomes and indicators, both for the organisation and for each of the individual groups affected. This is the point when a decision has probably been taken regarding whether to undertake the work in-house, or whether to use an external provider; whether or not to accredit the learning; and how assessment might contribute to the programme.

This chapter will consider how to develop the capacity within the organisation to deliver the WBL. It will explore some of the roles of the providers and commissioners and the degree to which the organisation will design the WBL programme. Factors that help learning to occur in the workplace will be discussed, as well as the implications for the workplace as identified in the eight critical success factors in Chapter One, should the learning be unsuccessful for individuals. Issues around assessment will be revisited in the light of workplace assessment rather than in relation to accreditation.

Prior to delivering the learning, the final part of the planning process concerns nailing down the details of the plan in practice. This is about designing the actual learning to be covered and commissioning its provision. Resources (people, money, time) will need to be allocated, their appropriate use determined, and the capacity to deliver created. This final stage involves the practical aspects of putting things in place to support the plan, including the supervision and assessment infrastructure and process.

Roles in the process

It can help to consider the roles in the design and implementation process and how this creates a WBL team. This is as important where a learning provider has been commissioned as when the work is carried out in-house, in order to avoid confusion over who is doing what and also to maintain a stakeholder approach. The learning team at its minimum should include the commissioner, the education provider and representation from the workforce, perhaps a manager from the appropriate department and, if possible, a learner representative. It may be appropriate to include representation from the unions or human resources to ensure that organisational policies are adhered to, for example to ensure consistency with study-time release, or implications for learning new skills for specific job roles.

This final planning can also be used to highlight where responsibilities are shared, so that a process can be developed which links roles together. The learning content or curriculum should be determined by discussions between the commissioner and provider so that they are in agreement as to what is required. Assessment, for example, is likely to require both organisational and provider input, and the details of this will agree what the assessment infrastructure is, who does what, and who and how quality will be assured. Additionally, if the outcome of assessment could result in changed job roles, or if failure means that jobs cannot stay the same, then human resources will need to be involved so that this is communicated appropriately to the worker–learners.

Figure 5.1 below details all the roles in a typical WBL programme. Managers will need to agree what each role/person brings to the table. This exercise can make a useful contribution to stakeholder evaluation. There may be overlap or duplication of roles in places due to job responsibilities.

This pie chart shows roles in the design process within the health sector. How would that look in your sector?

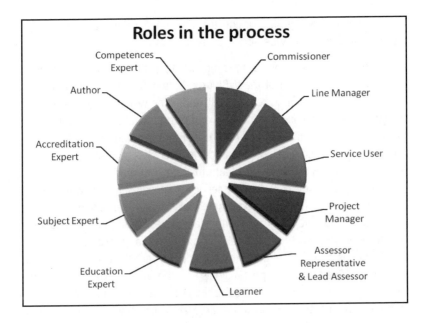

1. Commissioner (could also be the project manager)

2. Line manager of learner(s)

3. Service user

4. Project manager (or learning development team manager)

5. Assessor representative and lead assessor

6. Learner (either as co-educational designer or service user)

7. Education expert (provides education framework or overall programme of learning)

8. Subject expert (e.g. clinical nurse specialist, teacher or engineer)

9. Accreditation expert (may also be the education expert), e.g. FE/HE or professional body

10. Author (the person who writes the detailed programme) – this could also be the education expert

11. Expert on competences

For some WBL programmes, design team members or educational development teams may be added as extra roles.

All of these roles are involved, to some extent, in the detailed design and practical implementation of the WBL programme. Some of these roles will concern those commissioning WBL and some will be more about the process of designing the learning and/or accreditation. Each WBL programme is likely to need a different team, depending on whether an external provider is being used and the level of complexity of the learning programme. The design team may need to meet several times if the learning is complex. A client or service user representative will add a different perspective to the programme development. For example, some organisations have focus groups with clients to ascertain their perceptions about the service, such as for a television and media service, or the client's needs as in a local authority considering service provision for older residents. The education expert may also be the subject expert depending on the learning provider, or the accreditation expert may also be involved in designing competences, so some representatives may fulfil several roles. Not all WBL programmes are competence based, but there often is an element of practice capability required as an outcome of WBL.

What needs to be in place to support delivery?

In Chapter One, eight factors were identified as being critical to the success of the WBL programme. These were:

- Partnership
- Involvement of learners
- Leadership
- Outcomes
- Infrastructure
- Facilitation and support
- Capacity and capability
- Evaluation.

These will be explored specifically in relation to supporting the delivery of a WBL programme.

1. Partnership with the provider

Most organisations are likely to involve providers at this stage. When negotiating the finer details of the WBL contract, commissioners and providers can find that defining responsibility for details in the process is difficult to think through. The key questions for both parties will be "what is in their minds?" and "what do they mean by WBL?" The starting point will be the detailed outcomes required from the programme, since the aim of the learning will be to support and deliver them. Time spent with the education provider at this stage is likely to lead to better outcomes for the learners, and therefore more than one meeting is likely to be necessary.

Agreement will need to be reached about the overall features required, and whether any competence-based targets are to be achieved. The learning may be built around these as the provider may already have relevant modules which achieve this. Alternatively, the learning can be packaged so that groups of competences are addressed. There is likely to be some ongoing discussion in the development stage to ensure that the programme is progressing along the right track and that the provider has interpreted the organisation's specification and expectations appropriately. Failure to be explicit at the early stages can lead to misunderstandings and difficulties during the programme itself.

2. Involving learners

It has already been suggested that learners are included as stakeholders in the early stages of considering WBL. The best programmes make learners full partners in the process, and some providers are so clear about the importance of this that learning plans are increasingly individualised and follow initial self-evaluation or orientation modules. Currently, much under-16 compulsory education is developing and working within learner-centred paradigms, and this is likely to lead to increasing expectations of active involvement from a new generation of workers.

Additionally, if learners are involved in clarifying the objectives of the learning, they are likely to feel greater ownership of the outcomes and to feel included in the delivery of them. Also, learners can be central to working through how the learning can be delivered, and are well placed to spot potential learning opportunities. In many professions now, continuous professional development (CPD) includes designing learning contracts or programmes for individualised professional development, and consequently personal learning through a reflective process is expected to be a regular practice. It certainly offers opportunities for learners to capture learning from practice situations such as teamwork, work projects or encounters with clients. It may take the form of 'critical incident analysis' – where a problem is analysed and reviewed to ascertain what worked and the issues that arose from it – or 'appreciative enquiry' which can reflect upon why something was particularly effective or had a positive outcome.

3. Leadership

Leadership of the learning project should be undertaken by someone in the organisation who has project management skills, an understanding of the need for educational and training development and who appreciates the additional resources required to be effective. However, this person must also recognise that WBL is an investment in the organisation that (usually) cannot be provided by other means, resulting in benefits that are often long term rather than immediate.

The leader needs to have the authority to agree the details within the contract and an understanding of how it will impact on the daily work of the organisation. It is also helpful if there is some administrative support in relation to coordinating meetings between the partners, monitoring of the programme once it is running and communications with participants regarding practical details such as venues, timetabling, mentoring and assessors. This role may entail the maintenance of records of attendance and the monitoring or assessment of attendees' progress, thus requiring both control of detail and the authority to initiate. This type of information will also enable a subsequent audit trail to determine if the outcomes of the learning have been achieved, if there have been subsequent changes in practice or outcomes, and therefore if the investment has had an appropriate return.

4. Outcomes

As discussed earlier, the outcomes of the WBL should be measurable – both those of the programme that is to be achieved, and also those that indicate the effectiveness of the learning. Both of these will need monitoring during the programme of delivery to ensure that the learning is making a difference to the predetermined outcome measures. The leader of the overall learning project may be responsible for monitoring both of these, but the data is likely to be gathered from different quarters, and the mechanism for that needs to be put in place as part of the delivery programme. The education provider should be able to demonstrate how participants' views of the programme will be fed back to the commissioner as it progresses, and how the learners' experience is valued and used beyond superficial comments on whether the day's training was satisfactory.

5. Infrastructure

This involves a range of activities such as release from the workplace to attend development sessions, and the adjustment of work allocation to allow staff availability for development, including cover for staff release. It may also mean setting up specific training programmes for supervisors, assessors or mentors in order to allow learning from the workplace to be provided on an individual basis. This can help staff who have been in positions for some time to add new skills to their repertoire and discover that they like developing others, or that they have specific abilities in helping others to develop. A register of development and staff capability is a useful resource for managers to maintain to ensure allocation of development opportunities is fair and equitable.

There may also need to be a review of training on release practices, so that all workers get the same opportunities to develop new skills. Studies have shown that workers at management level are more likely to be sponsored by their managers for professional development than workers doing lower level and less responsible roles. In line with the national agenda for developing the workforce to higher skills levels, it may be that an organisation will need to review how professional development time is allocated. Some organisations will give time off but not pay for external courses; others may pay for courses but not allow staff paid time in which to do them, expecting them to adjust work patterns around them. This is where it is useful for a consistent policy to be in place for all to refer to within an organisation. Additionally, it should be remembered that there are a number of ways WBL can be provided within work time and that these may provide adequate training and development for some roles. Other types of WBL are discussed in Chapter Two.

6. Facilitation and support

As noted in Chapter One, managing WBL is an ongoing process and WBL programmes may be just one way of providing professional development for workers. Whilst the learner needs to be motivated to pursue the programme, the rest of the department may also need to be supportive and ideally the local ethos should encourage colleagues to undertake development. However, there must also be equal opportunities to participate. In some cases where colleagues are participating on the same programme, there may be a degree of competitiveness between them, which may need to be managed to ensure it does not adversely affect other work relationships.

Provision of training and education in the workplace may provide workers with the opportunity to revisit education which they might not have previously considered as an option open to them, particularly those who left school with few qualifications, or who have family or caring responsibilities that would otherwise take their spare time. Previous educational failure, disenchantment or disappointment may be an initial deterrent and some effort may be required from the provider or mentor to encourage perseverance and ensure success. Quite often, those who did not enjoy school find WBL more motivating and interesting because the applicability to their work role is more obvious, and success may mean promotion. This often results in more personal motivation towards their work as a whole and consequently may have a positive impact on other areas of their work role.

Failure to achieve or complete WBL can have a detrimental effect on an individual, and an impact on whether they remain in their work role. This possibility needs to be considered by the organisation before sending workers on WBL. If WBL is being used as a remedial process to improve staff working practices, then it should be clear to the staff that this is the reason that they are being sent on the programme. Failure to do this may result in no change of behaviour and reluctance to attend WBL, with a consequent impact on the rest of the job, misuse of development time and other resources. If WBL is used for managing workers who are underperforming, as an alternative to constructive managerial processes, the results will not be as effective as when WBL is used to upskill workers who are keen and eager to learn and develop their skills with a view to personal and organisational progression.

7. Capacity and capability

Building staff capability requires an ongoing awareness of staff development needs, of which the education provided by the WBL programme may be just one. A study (Portwood, 2000) in the early 1990s demonstrated that, whilst workers were appointed to their roles because of their experience and qualifications, once in post they had to learn in order to improve their proficiency and knowledge to stay in the role. This requires continuous learning within and about work, and so they thereby become 'work-based learners' just by doing their job. As a worker becomes more proficient they will engage with new skills, abilities and knowledge required for the role and expand to fit the required remit – and in many cases, beyond that remit. Limiting their role expansion will limit learning opportunities, but the best learning opportunities should be explicit and guided so that the individual can engage with them purposefully. Sharing skills and knowledge with other departments through project work or problem solving provides learning for a range of colleagues and encourages the development of capability and skill building across team boundaries.

Building capacity requires a similar approach in terms of sharing knowledge within teams and between roles so that there is overlap and inherent opportunities for individual development. The simple act of shadowing a senior colleague through a particular project or activity will provide a skilled deputy to cover holidays and sickness, and prepare a less-experienced individual to grow into a new role, thus creating succession planning through WBL.

One way to identify and capture potential capacity is to develop a competence framework for specific roles within an organisation. This may involve individuals sharing the knowledge that they have gained over a number of years and demonstrating their expertise and deep understanding of an organisation. This is often termed intellectual and human capital (Garnett, 2001) and is one of the greatest resources that an organisation has available. In WBL terms, this knowledge is often hidden to the outsider, and is termed 'tacit' knowledge (Eraut, 2001). It is at the fingertips of an individual but hard to articulate. Some WBL projects undertaken as part of a WBL programme can extract this sort of knowledge and make it available for the rest of the organisation. It is invaluable because it can reflect years of experience of key individuals and is then available to a wider audience.

8. Evaluation

Evaluation of WBL will go beyond the learner's initial response to one development day and should consider the impact and effectiveness of the learning, for the individual, the organisation, the clients and the provider. Using a structured approach to commissioning the WBL will aid and inform the evaluation process. Evaluation is discussed in more detail in the following chapter.

Using e-learning creatively

New technology can offer possibilities in learning provision. A factor to consider in WBL is the change of role of teacher–educator, which becomes one of facilitator and enabler of learning. If this role is seen as one which is shared jointly by organisations and providers, creative opportunities to enable learning can be built into programmes at organisational level. For example, could distance learning provide any element of the programme? What are the opportunities for engaging with e-learning in a creative way? Does the provider have expertise in this, or are both parties able to collaborate successfully here to design something new? Is there the technological infrastructure within the organisation to support this? If the provider offers it, can it be accessed through the work IT systems or will ICT-system security settings prevent easy access?

Different ways of working may need to be considered, as time and cost constraints may not permit a model where meetings are regular, or where full attendance is required. For example, some of the work may be carried out via a blog, a wiki, or social network sites, through video conferencing or meetings conducted through Skype (a free service that supports face-to-face conversations through the Internet). Virtual learning environments (VLEs), such as that used by the Open University, can be accessed free online, but will need technical support from inside the organisation. Examples of these are developing all the time and there are independent providers of VLEs that may be appropriate if the organisation is undertaking a significant investment in online development.

However, sustainable relationships need to be developed between partners in the WBL process. This may require face-to-face meetings, at least at first, in order for people to get to know and understand each other. HE providers report that people often feel lonely undertaking WBL. To support learners it can be helpful to include Action Learning Sets, or use social networking sites to provide a space for learners to share and discuss issues. Ways and modes of learning may not be classroom based and learners may not even meet each other or the educational provider physically. The use of such technology needs to be considered in relation to the age range and technological expertise of the workforce as it may prove too daunting for those who are unused to using computers to learn; whereas those who have left education relatively recently will have study expectations that certainly include ICT in some shape or form, especially if the job role requires computer literacy.

Developing an Action Plan to deliver WBL

The following checklist might be useful for constructing a detailed plan of action for the WBL programme:

- Are specific competence frameworks involved and who is designing/has designed these? Are they fit for purpose?

- Where is the learning to be delivered? When and what learning events will be held?

- How will the learner be involved in planning?

- How much time out is required for the learner?

- What kind of work-based support will be expected, e.g. are practical education staff in place on site? What staff can support the WBL and have they time?

- What resources will be included? e.g. ICT, library, work space for studying…

- Who will service resources such as websites?

- Who will be involved in assessment, who will do it and how will they be prepared?

- How will the outcomes for the learning be measured for the individual and the organisation? What criteria will be used?

- Who will supervise the learners? Will there be separate roles of mentors and assessors?

- Who will train any mentors? To what level? Do explicit guidance and expectations exist?

- What happens to a learner's job if they fail?

- Are responsibilities clearly defined and allocated to cover every aspect? Who is overseeing the WBL programme internally and externally? When and what meetings will be held by the steering group?

- Who is paying and at what stage(s)? How much?

Disseminating learning within the organisation

Increasingly organisations are looking to maximise investment in learning by ensuring that learners have an opportunity to feed back their learning to the wider organisation.

There are various levels of feedback which may be valuable, such as:

- To the purchasers and providers, regarding the fitness for purpose of the process itself

- From learners to others in their team/organisation, thus sharing learning and new ideas/skills gained

- From learners into the WBL-evaluation process.

Sometimes, learners are developed into roles, or they may extend them. However, where people have been developed out of their job/role, an action plan might be needed to ensure that skills are retained within the organisation.

Demonstrating achievement; using assessment effectively

Assessment in WBL should be focused around the required outcomes of the programme. For example, if a particular skill such as customer service is required, then that should form part or all of the assessment. However, it is important to design assessment which is not over complex or that involves too much assessment of individual elements. Assessment needs to be weighted in line with the level of the qualification. Well planned and simple assessment will be aided by a unified approach so that resources are not duplicated unnecessarily. Therefore, to ensure that WBL meets the identified needs, assessment design is crucial to ensure that it is fit for purpose and for practice.

In the previous chapter the overall context of assessment was considered and these questions were raised:

- Who is responsible for developing the assessment strategy?

- How will it be developed?

- Is there room for joint assessment with other initiatives, to conserve resources?

- What resources can be made available for assessment within the organisation?

- What skills will the assessors need to have, and are they already in place?

- Can a dedicated member of staff coordinate assessment?

At this stage, the practicalities of assessment for organisations in developing a detailed assessment plan and in delivering it are considered further. A sound starting point is to reflect on whether organisations should assess at all.

Who should assess?

Where an external learning provider is used, the overall assessment framework will need to meet the needs of any accrediting body, as well as the organisation, and this is likely to have an impact on the type of assessment designed. However, assessment of work-based skills is best undertaken by those closest to the practical outcomes of the learning, namely supervisors and others with whom the learner is in close contact. Assessment of academic skills is best undertaken by someone with understanding of the academic requirements.

Assessment can coordinate the input of staff with whom the learner is in contact: managers, other tutors, coaches, supervisors, practice facilitators, assessors, mentors and college staff, peers and even clients or customers in some industries. Ideally, responsibility for assessment should be shared between staff in the learner's organisation and staff from the education providers. These staff have many more opportunities for spotting where and whether learning is demonstrated, or not. They are in a good position to see whether the outcomes of learning are translated into practice, or capability. Peers can be included in the assessment process, although this needs to be designed with care and sensitivity to ensure that it is positive and constructive. Formal assessment personnel should facilitate this approach; in some circumstances this would include assessors external to the organisation.

Methods of assessment

Organisations can also benefit from becoming involved in designing the methods which are to be used for assessment. Methods of assessing learning (assessment activities) have developed greatly in recent years. Some methods offer many more opportunities for assessing competence rather than theoretical knowledge, and are therefore of greater interest to employers. The examples below represent some of those assessment methods that are particularly appropriate for the workplace:

- Seminar or presentation to colleagues
- Direct and indirect observations
- Oral exams

- Work-based projects, either individual or team

- Reports (which may also be those required for the workplace)

- Case studies, actual or simulated

- Research projects

- Reflective essays summarising personal learning and integration of new theoretical understanding into practice

- Formative exercises to allow feedback and redrafting

- Portfolios of evidence with commentary

- Videos of practice behaviour

- Role play or simulation exercises.

Traditional methods of assessment such as exams or written essays are usually discouraged as the linkage to work practice is not always made explicit and it is the application to the work environment which is the key to effective WBL assessment. Some external programmes from education providers will have specific assessments that must be completed, such as NVQs or validated modules from FE or HE. However, if these do not reflect organisational needs then it may be possible to renegotiate these for specific requirements.

Every method of assessment has its strengths and weaknesses, and therefore a range of assessments is best used in order to obtain the best assessment results. For example, using two or more forms of assessment can provide an opportunity to test different skills and knowledge and thus strengthen the robustness of the assessment process. Research indicates that some types of learners perform better in different types of assessment and therefore that some methods of assessment are more suited to some learners than others, even within the same programme. Furthermore, some forms of assessment might disadvantage dyslexic or otherwise-disabled learners, and this has implications for the type of learner and WBL programme that is being used.

Whilst the use of information technology (ICT) is proceeding at a rapid rate and is increasingly used within assessment, it may not constitute a method in itself. Examples of this are the use of phrases such as 'e-assessment' or 'online assessment', which are really *tools* of assessment rather than methods in themselves. Some new assessment methods are likely to be formed through the use of ICT, but this should be designed to achieve the learning outcomes. For example, the use of an online quiz may test underpinning knowledge, and may be supplemented by a real-life case study or simulated exercise demonstrating the application of knowledge in practice and also showing the extent to which the new learning is embedded.

Most methods of assessment can be used to assess varying levels of learning/skill. For example:

- A work-based project can ask a learner to demonstrate skills in description, analysis, information gathering and sifting and critical thinking

- A practical demonstration/simulation will enable the learner to demonstrate competence in a procedure

- A presentation to peers will demonstrate communication skills, as well as showing a range of colleagues the depth of learning that has been achieved through a particular learning activity.

An understanding and a little background knowledge of the types of assessment that may be available, particularly for newly designed WBL, can help ensure informed purchase where necessary. Hardacre and Masterson (2007) offer a full list of assessment methods used in the health sector and this has some general applicability outside of health. Methods are described, together with a brief assessment of their strengths and weaknesses, drawn from wider research.

Assessment in WBL should be applicable to the workplace. It involves embedding new knowledge, skills and attitudes and is therefore often performance related. Assessing attitudes and behaviour is a speciality of WBL, and is important as these often influence work practice, which may need to be changed after development or education. For example, customer-service development or disability awareness courses should impact on how staff behave. Quite often workplace assessment is easier to manage if it is just 'pass' or 'fail' rather than graded, as practice skills are either competent or not and having to grade them adds an additional layer of complexity for the assessor. This is easier for written work also as it can eliminate some competitive elements between colleagues.

An important principle is that the assessor may be a member of the workforce, but should not be in direct line management of the learner. There should be a degree of objectivity and a different line of accountability. Particularly for practical skills, a WBL learner may have several observers at different stages of their learning activity, but ideally the assessor should be constant. Sometimes there might be two assessors making assessment judgments, but in that case there should be explicit guidelines so that expectations are clear, and the opportunity to confer should be available. For example, the use of competences may require more than one assessor in different parts of the organisation making judgments, but only one set of criteria for consistency.

The mode of assessment must reflect:

- The resources available
- The outcomes required for practice
- The amount of new knowledge required as evidence.

Success and progression

Some assessment approaches reject the idea of 'failure' and encourage the notion of relearning until achievement is satisfactory. This is particularly so in the culture of NVQs. However, when WBL moves into HE and FE levels and academic skills are required, the concept of failure has to be considered. Ideally failure should not have negative connotations for the actual job role so that the learner does not have to fear for their job security if they cannot pass.

However, they may not be able to progress through certain promotions or to a role that they covet if they do not pass and this can have implications for performance in assessment. Some may be tempted to copy another's notes or assignments or get information from the Internet. In HE this is seen as plagiarism and poor practice, and can result in a learner being removed from a programme. Interestingly, experience indicates that plagiarism is more difficult to achieve on a WBL course because the outcomes are so specific to a given workplace that unoriginal work is easily identified by the assessors. However, learners may plagiarise unwittingly through weak academic referencing skills and programmes provided by colleges should ensure that basic study skills address this at the outset of a programme, if relevant to the end product. For example, in a written WBL project report that requires the use of new theory, the learners should learn how to incorporate it into their written work in a way that meets academic expectations.

Failure to learn new skills and complete competences will have a detrimental effect on WBL learners and this possibility needs to be anticipated by the organisation so that appropriate measures can be written into the course materials. If necessary, discussions with unions or managers should be undertaken to prepare for this so remedial interventions can be devised and then, where necessary, implemented. It is vital therefore that organisations and education providers do not set learners up to fail by demanding skills and WBL activities that are inappropriate or beyond the learner's capability, or that cannot be accommodated within the WBL programme. It is also important that expectations from the learning programme are made explicit so that all involved know what the outcomes are and how they will be addressed. For an organisation unused to such educational requirements this may take some time to develop, therefore close working with the education provider will be an important part of the negotiation process.

Collegial rivalry may emerge during a WBL programme and have a negative impact upon work relationships (Rounce, 2009). Whilst this does not directly lead to failure, it may result in strained work relationships and misunderstandings between colleagues. If a group project is required, as is often the case because real WBL projects involve a team, then there may be difficulties regarding work allocation and equality of contribution within that project. This should be dealt with by the education provider as part of the explicit WBL programme requirements. Ideally it should not affect the workplace itself, but the organisation should be aware of this.

Developing a detailed assessment plan

- Who will assess and how?

- What methods are appropriate? How will it apply to practice?

- Will a mixed method of assessment capture the full range of new learning or a single mode?

- Is online assessment possible or appropriate? If so who will design, deliver and assess it?

- What support will be available for learners (external; internal)?

- What are the associated mentoring/supervision requirements, and therefore development implications and ICT-infrastructure requirements?

- What resources are required? Who will provide them? The commissioner? The provider?

- How are the responsibilities for location and time out for assessment to be apportioned?

The main considerations in this chapter have revolved around the organisation recognising factors that support the practicalities of learning in the workplace, and identifying where and how to address these factors so that learning opportunities can be maximised.

References

Eraut, M. (2001) 'The role and use of vocational qualifications', *National Institute Economic Review*, 78, 88–98

Garnett, J. (2001) 'Work Based Learning and the Intellectual Capital of Universities and employers', *The Learning Organisation*, 8 (2), 78–81

Hardacre, K. and Masterson, A. (2007) *Exploring Best Practice in the Assessment of Competence in the Health Sector*, report available from Skills for Health

Portwood, D. (2000) 'An intellectual case for Work Based Learning as a subject', in Portwood, D. and Costley, C. (2000) *Work based Learning and the University: New Perspectives and Practices*, SEDA paper 109, Birmingham

Rounce, K. (2009) 'Partnerships in Higher Education', in Garnett, J., Costley, C., and Workman, B. (2009) *Work Based Learning: Journeys to the Core of Higher Education*, MU Press, London

CHAPTER SIX

Evaluating the plan

Why evaluate Work Based Learning?

Development costs can be significant in any business. Most employers are prepared to incur these costs because they expect their business or their clients to benefit from employees' development and progress. The exact bill for training and development in the UK is not known since so many individuals and organisations contribute to it, and it is measured in widely differing ways. However, Leitch (2006) notes that:

> employers, individuals and the Government all invest significantly in skills improvements. In England, employers spend around £2.4 billion on direct course costs and up to £17.4 billion in total, excluding the wages of employees. Employer investment in skills varies significantly by type of employee, type of employer and sector of the economy.... The Government in England invests around £12 billion on adult skills each year, of which around £4.5 billion is on further education (FE), including work-based learning, and £7.4 billion on higher education (HE). These are the overall costs of tuition, learner support and capital. Individuals will pay £1.35 billion per annum through the new variable tuition fees, on top of the existing £0.9 billion per annum income from standard fees.

> (Leitch, 2006: 12)

Given these figures, it is perhaps surprising that so little training and development has been subject to evaluation. In the past, employers often overlooked evaluation, perhaps because the benefits, particularly financial ones, can be hard to describe in concrete terms. Time constraints are often mentioned. Where evaluation has taken place, it is often designed after learning programmes have finished, when it is least effective.

There are, though, good reasons for evaluating learning. Evaluation can help to:

- Track the development of staff knowledge and skills

- Find out if the learning is being applied in the workplace

- Establish the cost effectiveness of investment

- Improve similar future initiatives

- Identify development gaps and future development needs

- Inform future development plans and strategy.

The process of evaluation can also act as a learning resource in itself, especially where multiple stakeholders are involved. Involvement in evaluation of learning communicates a clear message to staff that the development of skills and knowledge is treated seriously. Over recent years the growth in value for money concepts and an improvement in business planning procedures in the public sector has led to evaluation becoming more common. This can be evidenced through the increasing numbers of consultants offering evaluation services. However, experts in evaluation, even if well informed and rewarded, can only evaluate development or learning which has a clear purpose from the outset. That is, unless the client is clear what benefit was intended from the learning, it is not possible for anyone to identify with any clarity whether the aims have been achieved.

Evaluation which is 'tagged on' with hindsight is problematic for a number of reasons, not least because people tend to see their past or original intentions differently over time. Some organisations are now seeing the benefit of growing evaluation expertise in-house, partly because of cost but also because of the benefits associated with insider knowledge of staff and processes. Evaluation advice is likely to be offered in advance of work commencing, when it is most useful. As a result, the Internet advertises quite a few in-house self-evaluation courses.

Organisations with experience of evaluation are keen to ensure that it is planned in advance and well designed, that it uses time wisely and that its scale is in proportion to the benefits envisaged.

The five evaluation levels or domains

The four commonly quoted evaluation domains were first described by Kirkpatrick and Kirkpatrick (2007). They consider:

- **The reaction of students** – what they thought and felt about the development

- **Learning** – the resulting increase in knowledge or capability

- **Behaviour** – the extent of behaviour and capability improvement and implementation/application

- **Results** – the effects on the business or environment resulting from the trainee's performance.

These are useful domains, because they provide a framework for moving well beyond the 'happy sheet' approach, which simply measures student reaction. It also allows us to see immediately that different evaluation domains might require a different approach. The Kirkpatrick domains are normally considered as successive evaluation levels (levels 1–4).

There is an excellent discussion about the Kirkpatrick model, with examples of each level, an assessment of each, and references, on the businessballs website (www.businessballs.com).

A fifth domain is commonly added: **Return on Investment (or ROI)**. This aims to determine the margin of benefit in relation to cost. Return on investment can help to quantify the cost versus benefit of WBL, using in part a mathematical formula. It focuses on the cost benefit of the development, or the extent (in financial terms) to which benefits exceed cost. This seems attractive, since one of the reasons the development budget is often the first casualty of a recession is that the financial or tangible benefits of it are unclear.

However, some people find ROI complex to understand, and time consuming to apply. Recent critics have pointed out that where cost benefit analyses are applied to development, it is impossible to be certain that factors other than cost, e.g. human factors, will not cloud results. Of those people applying this formula, most are likely to have complex and costly, often national, projects and programmes of work to evaluate.

A further problem for ROI is that outcomes are only as reliable as the financial data used to calculate them. It can be difficult to cost or ascribe value to some things accurately. For example, design time is a cost, but does it include only the formal, planned time set aside for design and write up, or should an element be added for thinking time? However, ROI is useful for focussing the mind on what aspects of learning might be measured. The following list indicates the types of costs and benefits which are typically measured, although each evaluation team will wish to add its own:

Costs
- Design and development
- Administration
- Management
- Teaching materials
- Equipment
- Direct learner costs
- Time lost from workplace
- Educational consultancy

Benefits
- Increased productivity
- Improved performance
- Savings on business costs
- Reduction in sick leave
- Reduction in staff turnover
- Other benefits e.g. to the client or consumer group

Other issues to consider include the source of the data, and how it will be measured. How subjective will this be? If external providers are used for part of the work, what will they cost? In terms of the balance between cost and benefits, are the possible costs of implementing ROI likely to outweigh the benefits of the learning evaluation exercise?

Clarifying the purpose of the evaluation

Robson (2000) lists nine questions commonly asked of research evaluation, and suggests that the ones relevant to each evaluation will, in turn, suggest particular processes to adopt. He states that most evaluations are asking one or more of the following:

1. What is needed?

2. Does what is provided meet client needs?

3. What happens when it is in operation?

4. Does it attain its goals or objectives?

5. What are its outcomes?

6. How do costs and benefits compare?

7. Does it meet required standards?

8. Should it continue?

9. How can it be improved?

Robson states that different subsets of these questions will be central to different evaluations. Using the model proposed in this chapter means that the type of WBL programme will be chosen with learning needs in mind at the outset; but where learning is evaluated, most of these questions can be addressed.

Some of the answers will already be known to these questions. This is because:

- A **needs analysis** will have been carried out (Chapter Three)

- Anticipated **costs and benefits** have been worked through(Chapter Three)

- An **overall outcome** for the learning was set (Chapter Three)

- The **detailed objectives and outcomes** expected of the learning were determined (Chapter Four)

- Consideration was given in advance to what might indicate success and **how the outcomes would be measured** (Chapter Four)

- Key **stakeholders have been identified**, who share ownership of the outcomes, have been consulted, and any differences of viewpoint resolved.

The emphasis for the evaluation is measuring whether those outcomes have been attained, and to capture that learning for future initiatives. Therefore this is an evaluation of outcomes, although that does not preclude the capture of useful information about process during the project.

Getting the balance right

All too often evaluation is at a superficial level, offering information only about basic issues such as immediate learner satisfaction as in 'how was it for you?' However, time and resources are scarce commodities in workplaces. For this reason, when designing evaluation, it is important to decide in advance the scale of the evaluation required.

It pays to achieve a balance between the scale of the evaluation and the size, scope or importance of the learning being evaluated. It is not effective to design an evaluation which is costly in terms of the time it takes for staff to contribute, if the aim of the original learning is not considered critical to business success. In conditions where budgets are restricted, learning is usually considered critical, or it is not commissioned.

For instance, it might appear to be wise for a hospital to concentrate more effort on ensuring that infection-control training has been effective than in carrying out an in-depth evaluation of a short mentoring course. The impact on core business is more obvious. But poor mentoring may have a negative impact on the quality of staff performance, and that has a lasting effect on the next five years of graduates and their clients. A local authority might think it wise to evaluate the effectiveness of learning on a project management course for a single individual, if that individual will have responsibility for rebuilding the authority's schools, at enormous cost. Even simple evaluation, when well chosen, can save money and time. Therefore the case for not evaluating has a limited currency if the longer-term impact is considered.

There may well be some extra benefit to developing longer-term relationships with some external evaluation services, such as education providers who can be expected to contribute to the evaluation costs in some way, perhaps as part of a larger research project, such as in sharing ownership of the results, not least in terms of winning future learning contracts with their clients. Further practical ideas to help with managing time constraints are mentioned in the discussion of stakeholder evaluation below.

Getting started

The main areas to think about for deciding the design parameters of evaluation are:

- The key evaluation question being addressed

- Who to involve (number, who to include and exclude)

- The timescale for the evaluation

- How the data will be collected, and

- Which sources of data will reveal the most useful information most quickly or effectively.

For our purposes, the evaluation question is likely to be asking whether or not outcomes determined earlier have been met. Evaluation using the previously identified stakeholders will make a significant contribution.

Stakeholders as evaluators

As previously stated, stakeholders are those people and organisations who may affect, be affected by, or perceive themselves to be affected by a decision or activity. There is a discussion on defining stakeholders in Chapter Four, because of the added value and increased ownership of including stakeholders from the start. Some organisations now prefer to implement stakeholder evaluation models, using stakeholders to design the parameters of the evaluation and even to carry it out.

Involving many stakeholders will help ensure that the evaluation process goes more smoothly because:

- More people have a 'stake' or interest in the outcomes of the learning

- A message is sent that the outcomes of the learning are taken seriously

- More people are prepared to consider and uncover the information required

- Project-staff concerns about the burden of evaluation can be reduced

- The information gathered is more reliable and comes from different perspectives, thus enabling contradictory information to be gathered and resolved

- The recommendations are likely to be accepted by a broader constituency and implemented more fully and with more support.

This method of evaluation has the benefit of collecting a wide range of views on the original intervention. It can be surprisingly objective, since views will be collected from a range of different stakeholders, who may see things differently from each other, thereby adding depth. It enables more clarity and agreement about what is needed from the intervention than is often the case.

In stakeholder evaluation, the overall coordinator of the learning or the evaluator takes on more of a role of facilitating the evaluation, rather than carrying it out directly, although he or she may take on some extra responsibilities, such as detailed design or writing reports. One of the reasons why stakeholder evaluation can be so valuable is because power, responsibility and involvement are handed over to its participants.

It is often difficult to persuade people to take part in evaluation exercises. As in many management activities, it is critical to success that people see the benefits to them of taking part. This is less difficult to present with stakeholder evaluation, since, by definition, the outcomes under evaluation are those the stakeholders designed and agreed.

The basic processes in stakeholder evaluation

Stakeholders can be involved in evaluation to a greater or lesser extent. We have already looked at the idea of grading stakeholders into those who are critical to success and those whom it is simply useful to involve. Some evaluation information is only available to certain stakeholders. This may not emerge at first, and new stakeholders might need to be added.

The main processes involved in stakeholder-led evaluation are:

1. Identifying who to include in the evaluation process (individuals or by group type)

2. Collecting and recording stakeholder expectations of the learning intervention, including priorities, to compare against the results in practice

(required outcomes)

3. Deciding what data to collect for evaluation purposes

4. Determining how data will be gathered and used

5. Setting the timescales by which results can be realistically collected

6. Implementing future changes.

These responsibilities are mainly managerial. However, some stakeholder evaluations go further than this, offering stakeholders more than a management role. For example, they may contribute to the design of the evaluation intervention more fully, particularly if they have specialist expertise.

An example might involve a WBL initiative to develop health and safety skills in an office environment. One specific impact measure could be "a reduction in accidents (or one type of accident) across the organisation during the next year". One person may collect this information or it may be held at individual office level. There may also be a number of sites involved, in which case it would be necessary to understand the existing data-collection arrangements. It might not even be collected! Some system reform would be necessary. It would need to be built in to the development project at the outset, probably the previous year, to enable its collection. There may be other ways to collect it without disruption.

Stakeholders may of course collect data directly. For large and complex multi-organisational projects, this may mean that individual stakeholder representatives delegate data collection and other tasks to others within the organisation they represent. It is worth spending some time agreeing minimal proformae or question sets to guide the data collection, so that the information is collected in a standard format. It would be possible to use a shared electronic space, such as a project space for a blog or wiki for recording results, to save on staff data collection-time.

A further role for stakeholders may be in the interpretation and analysis of evaluation results. Even where this is not desired, some group time can be set aside to consider the initially collated raw data, as opposed to drawing up detailed evaluation results and producing reports or briefings.

It will be necessary to have an overall coordinator or lead manager who will lead and coordinate the evaluation exercise, typically:

- Providing project-manager support – e.g. by managing the evaluation timescales and budget

- Carrying out the intervention

- Collecting evaluation results

- Writing up the evaluation results

- Coordinating the change intervention resulting from the evaluation

- Supporting the evaluation stakeholders throughout the process.

Managing stakeholder time

At a glance, stakeholder evaluation can look labour intensive, but it need not be. Once it is clear what stakeholders expect the WBL to achieve (their predictive expectations), they can be involved to a greater or lesser extent. They can be used for some parts of the process and not others. An analysis of time outlay for one project might look like this:

- Workshop to develop and agree detailed outcomes and their measures

- Workshop to discuss and design data collection (this could be a follow on session on the same day as the workshop above)

- Meeting to discuss results and agree implications for future

A small project might adapt the methodology in the following way:

- Video-recorded discussion of expectations for the project, finishing with individuals agreeing to think up outcome measures with colleagues and send them in to their manager

- Manager to write these up and circulate them for agreement by blog or email

- Final meeting, including learners and line managers (or relevant staff) to replay video and to debate the extent to which expectations were met

A large and complex project, such as a national workforce project, might devote much more time to developing and carrying out a stakeholder approach. Even then, existing steering and reference groups used by many projects can often be adapted for this purpose, making them more productive in many cases. Where much stakeholder activity is anticipated, advance planning will help. For example, a critical path or project plan detailing the activities involved in the evaluation can be agreed and circulated in advance, so that potential diary conflicts can be managed. An example project plan is included at the end of this chapter.

Some extra ideas on how to use stakeholders creatively are set out below.

- Make a stakeholder forum a part of your programme and evaluation

- Design an effective process in the learning project to implement change *during the course* of the learning, should the need arise

- On large projects, create a stakeholder blog and encourage its use, particularly by learners and assessors

- When asking stakeholders about the outcomes of learning critical to success, get them to prioritise (the fewer, the better)

- Make learners the key stakeholders

- For some specific learning projects, it can be illuminating to chart an organisational process or the key team activities before and after learning has taken place, to identify where the learning has been effective

We have found that involving stakeholders can increase the creativity of evaluation, as they are likely to suggest new ways in which they can be involved which had not previously been considered.

Timing data collection

Thought needs to be given to when data can be collected. Some evaluations are likely to call for data collection during the process of the learning programme, in order to test development over time, and to adapt the learning as necessary. This allows for the development of responsive and flexible learning. Unless a programme is large or complex, this is likely to be informal, and quick. To evaluate overall outcomes, data will be collected post intervention. This might not be immediate – timescales will emerge as the programme develops.

Referring to Chapter Two on the different types of learning commonly undertaken will guide the evaluation strategy as the type of learning approach will influence the evaluation approach. Evaluation might be immediately post programme, particularly for skills-based learning. The outcomes of the learning may provide evidence for evaluation, such as project reports indicating how successful the learning has been. Other kinds of learning, however, will need to be embedded before outcomes can be measured properly, so other dates by which results might be expected (e.g. one year, three years) will need to be built in. However, the pace of workplace change can make such a thorough approach problematic.

Evaluation results

Most evaluation findings are written up in report format. This is most useful for formal stakeholders, such as commissioners, as they may use it to support applications for further funding. Consideration can be given to producing and disseminating findings differently for other audiences, and adopting appropriate communication methods for these audiences. In addition, some individuals or groups will be more interested in some evaluation findings than others. Segmenting the audience, and producing different feedback for each, might make a key difference to whether the findings are utilised.

Lots of methods can be used to communicate findings, as well as various media. Formal reports are best produced in three versions: a full report, with an executive summary, and a third version entitled "what the findings mean for you", aimed at decision makers. Even with the main report, much can be consigned to appendices; nobody usually wants to read long and descriptive detail about process. Bullet points, PowerPoint presentations and short articles can be produced for other stakeholders. A powerful approach is the inclusion of 'narratives', short case-study illustrations, which demonstrate the effect of the intervention. However, it is important to complete this evaluation step even with non-critical stakeholders, both to share learning widely and to respect the time invested by contributors.

Stakeholders can influence outcomes in other ways, by supporting learning activity, as the following case study shows:

CASE STUDY

Case Study 1

A work-based learning project was set up at a large manufacturing company, with the involvement of the local university, to develop management skills in senior staff. It was decided that the stakeholders included the university staff, on-site managers, a client, and a number of people, including finance and HR representatives, with whom these staff worked. Two learners were also involved.

A project group was set up to consider what was needed from the development and how it would be evaluated, and when. The project manager summed up the benefits of involving stakeholders:

CASE STUDY

Everyone feels that their needs are understood, acknowledged, and taken into account – for instance the major client felt that the outcomes of the programme related to his needs, and therefore he was willing to make development opportunities available to participants throughout the learning. The finance manager facilitated shadowing and short secondment opportunities, which he may not otherwise have done, and this helped the staff to understand how they needed to work with finance staff, and why... sort of, how it all fits together.

Some stakeholders will contribute views which will change the nature of what you are trying to achieve in the first place, and they are less likely to say afterwards that this sort of training is a waste of time.

The university staff were happy that staff involvement in the learning itself was greater than they normally experienced, and they thought that lots of usually theoretical learning was able to be grounded in practical reality, and interpreted for this part of the manufacturing sector.

We think that stakeholders often provided extra pairs of hands with both the intervention and with the evaluation, because they have been involved from the beginning, and therefore the 'ownership', that we sometimes pay lip service to, becomes real, and useful for everyone.

Summary

Evaluating learning is not a difficult process. It can offer a chance for reflection, and it is possible to design it as an organic and integral part of a programme. It can make a real difference to the path which particular programmes take. It can offer opportunities for insights which suggest change as the project proceeds. It can become a learning tool for the manager and for the stakeholders involved, meaning that as others proceed in their careers they carry those skills with them. Finally, it makes a real difference to outcomes for future learners if lessons are implemented.

Two checklists for programme managers can be found in the appendices, which can help plan an evaluation from the beginning.

References

Businessballs website, www.businessballs.com (accessed March 2008)

Fryer, B. (2006) *Learning for a Change in Healthcare*, November 2006, www.wideningparticipation.nhs.uk (accessed March 2009)

Kirkpatrick, D.L. and Kirkpatrick, J.D. (2007) *Evaluating Training Programmes: The four levels (Third edition)*

Leitch, S. (2006) *Prosperity for all in the global economy – world class skills*, HMSO, Norwich

Pullman Phillips, J. and Phillips, J.J. (2005) *Return on Investment Basics*, American Society of Training and Development, ASTD Press

Robson, C. (2000) *Small Scale Evaluation,* Sage Publications Ltd

Good practice in stake-holder evaluation: checklist

Have you...	Yes	No	Dates/comments
Identified and rated your stakeholders?			
Confirmed and agreed the purpose of the learning intervention?			
Discussed the purpose of the evaluation (the 'expectations' of all from the WBL intervention)?			
Agreed your detailed evaluation objectives?			
Agreed detailed indicators for change you will seek to measure?			
Resolved any differences of view between your stakeholders?			
Decided how you will work together, and when?			
Agreed how and where information will be collected?			
Agreed who will help to collect the information?			
Decided who will analyse it?			
Agreed how it will be presented and how differences will be resolved?			
Agreed how and to whom you will present the final outcomes?			
Agreed a detailed timeframe and project plan, with processes, names, outcomes and dates?			
Agreed any necessary administrative support?			

APPENDIX TWO

Detailed project plan template

	Action	Outcome	Lead manager	Contributors	Timescale
1					
2					
3					

Index